THE BOG MEADOWS
THE RIVER BLACKSTAFF

Des O'Reilly

Published by Stranmillis University College, Belfast
© Des O'Reilly 2008

ISBN 978 0 903009 32 4

Front cover photograph by Richard Greenwood

Designed by April Sky Design, Newtownards
Printed by GPS Colour Graphics Limited, Belfast

April Sky Design
Colourpoint House
Jubilee Business Park
21 Jubilee Road
NEWTOWNARDS
County Down
Northern Ireland
BT23 4YH
Tel: 028 9182 7195
Fax: 028 9182 1900
E-mail: info@aprilsky.co.uk
Web site: www.aprilsky.co.uk

Foreword

The Blackstaff River has finally disappeared from view as the last stretch of the river between Stockman's Lane and Grosvenor Road has been culverted or diverted as part of the road developments along the West Link and MI. It brings to a successful conclusion the various attempts by different government and local authorities over the years to deal with the 'Blackstaff nuisance' by putting it underground. The role of the river in shaping the nature and extent of the Bog Meadows is now part of history as is its importance in providing the power needed for early industries along the banks of its tributaries. It may no longer be easily visible on the surface but frequently it breaks out of its concrete and steel pipes to flood the surrounding streets above ground as witnessed at the underpass at Broadway in 2008. The advent of global warming and rising seas levels may once again cause the Blackstaff to rise out of its containment and join the advancing estuarine waters to claim back the floodplain through which it meandered for many thousands of years.

Acknowledgements

I am extremely grateful to the staffs of the various institutions where I have accessed relevant material, especially the staffs of Stranmillis University College, Public Record Office of Northern Ireland, Ulster Wildlife Trust, Linenhall Library, Belfast, Central Library, Ulster Museum, Rivers Agency, British Library and National Library of Ireland.

My thanks to the following people who helped in various ways at different stages in its production, Alun Evans, Aidan Crean, Tim Duffy, Paul Riordan, Jim Cahill, Robin Livingstone, Eamonn Phoenix, Christine Kinealy and my former colleagues in St Mary's University College, Micheal McEntee and Peter Collins who along with Richard Greenwood of Stranmillis University College reviewed the earlier drafts.

I am greatly indebted to Cilla Wagner, Manager of the Learning Support Services of Stranmillis University College for her guidance and advice and her colleague, Cathy Brady who typed most of the text and for their careful stewartship of the project.

Much of the artwork has been done by my son, Desmond (Jnr) who drew on demand so expertly with his characteristic skill and attention to detail. In addition, I am grateful to my brother Sean, who inspired me with his stories about his childhood experiences in the Bog Meadows.

The author and publishers wish to thank the following for permission to reproduce material: Photograph of red and yellow sandstone outcrop at Milltown. Geological Survey of Northern Ireland. (Pg.2). Figs 9.1(pg.27), 9.2 (pg.28), 9.3 (pg.29), 10.4 (pg.35). Courtesy of Deputy Keeper of the Records, Public Record Office of Northern Ireland. Photograph of painting of Paper Mill, Belfast (1850) by James Moore, Courtesy the Trustees of National Museums Northern Ireland. Fig 10.1 (pg.31). Photograph of the painting of The Long Bridge, Belfast by Andrew Nichol, Courtesy of the Trustees of National Museums Northern Ireland. Fig. 10.2 (pg.32). Fig 12.1 (pg.45), 12.2 (pg.45). Courtesy Of the National Library of Ireland. Fig 13.1 (pg.49). Courtesy of History Ireland Photograph of flooding in Belfast, Courtesy of Belfast Telegraph (pg.72). Fig. 20.1 (pg. 69) Courtesy of the Trustees of the British Library Photograph of the 'Bog Meadow's Bachelor'. Courtesy of Andersonstown News (pg.40).

In some instances we have been unable to trace the owners of copyright material, and we would appreciate any information that would enable us to do so. Finally, I would like to record a more personal debt to my wife Ann and my children Fintan, Gerald, Desmond (Jnr), Fiona and Adrian. This book is dedicated to them.

Introduction

The few acres that constitute the Bog Meadows today are but a small percentage of the great marshy area that once almost surrounded the early town of Belfast from the Point Fields in the north to the estuarine shallows in the south. It consisted of meadowland and marsh, fields and open water through which the River Blackstaff flowed. It was an oasis of wildlife endowed with a wide range of habitats and floral diversity. During the summer months it came alive with an immense variety of insect species preyed on by a large number of insect-eating birds. It was the breeding ground of the corncrake. In winter it was the temporary home of migrating flocks of geese on their way to warmer climes.

Despite the idyllic nature of the setting it was too close the town of Belfast and its inhabitants to remain untouched from the demands of a rising populace.. Gradually as the town expanded haphazardly along the Falls and Lisburn Roads the Bog Meadows was confined to 400 acres of the flood plain by the year 1900. During the following hundred years this was reduced dramatically as roads and housing continued to impact on the remaining acreage.

This book traces the changes that have taken place over the many years beginning with the physical changes that occurred in glacial and pre-glacial times and ending with the final demise of the lowlands of the Blackstaff and the river with the widening of the M1 motorway and the West Link.

But the story of the Bog Meadows and Blackstaff lowlands is not confined to the physical make-up of the area but incorporates the various ways in which people who lived along the course of the Blackstaff exploited the river and surrounding marsh and meadow for various uses including

- The factory owner who used the power of the tributaries to drive the water wheels and machinery for the cotton and linen mills along the banks

- The farmer who raised cattle and pigs on the meadows and cut hay for the horses stabled in the town.

- The wildfowler who preyed on the geese , wild duck and snipe sprung from the rushes.

The growing needs of the expanding town prompted the Donegall family and a rising bourgeoisie to build institutions to attend to the needs of a growing populace. These institutions were mostly sited along the Falls and Lisburn Roads and by the end of the 19th century several were built along the edge of the Bog Meadows including a hospital for the sick, a lunatic asylum, a workhouse, an industrial school and an institution for the deaf and dumb. In later times schools for the young and cemeteries for the dead were added.

There is, however, a more human and personal side to the story of the Bog Meadows. As the population increased dramatically during the 19th century the core areas of the Lower Falls and Sandy Row pushed outwards and encroached further into the Bog Meadows and Blackstaff wetlands. The people from these new urban areas ventured into the fields and wetland areas for leisure activities, some following the traditions and customs of rural Ulster from which many migrated free from the brick and concrete confinement of the surrounding streets. Using personal accounts and anecdotes, various events and experiences are described, some amusing, some puzzling and some tragic.

The story ends with the diversion and culverting of the Blackstaff River under the M1 and Westlink in 2007 leaving only a remnant of the Blackstaff lowlands in the Nature Reserve as a testament to the past.

Contents

CHAPTER 1
Pre-Glacial Landscape

Deep down under the Bog Meadows there appears to be a narrow trench cut into beds of sandstone and mudstones by an ancient river system. Subsurface contours reveal that this ancient channel commences at a depth of ten metres at a point coincident with St Galls GAC grounds at Milltown on the surface and deepens in a north-east direction to a depth of 40 metres as it enters a down- faulted trough under Belfast Lough. Evans (1944) put forward the view that this ancient river channel represents the pre-glacial River Lagan of which the River Blackstaff was a tributary and that later glacial events prevented the Lagan from following the general direction of its old course which the modern Blackstaff occupied subsequently.

The beds of sandstone and mudstones which underlie the Bog Meadows belong to a series of sediments laid down in a geological period known as the Triassic (240-206 million years ago). During this period desert conditions prevailed and huge mountain chains were worn down progressively over vast time spans. Erosion of these mountains created immense masses of sediment which accumulated in the low lying basins and valleys brought down by wind and the occasional flash floods The earlier surface became covered with sand-dunes and coarse sediment washed in by torrential rivers. On the flat plains temporary lakes were formed which trapped the finer dust particles which blew constantly over this treeless landscape. This fine material accumulated on the floor of these water bodies and built up layer upon layer to form the mudstones that are now exposed.

The sandstones and mudstones which were formed in this desert are to be seen today in different outcrops in and around the Bog Meadows. The best exposure of the sandstone forms the steep bank at the top of the Rock streets from Rockville Street to the Giant's Foot at Beechmount. Few fossils have been found in these sandstones because of the harsh conditions that prevailed at the time, but there is one noted footprint of an early reptile that was discovered in the sandstones of Scrabo quarry Co.Down. Perhaps the Giant's Foot got its name from the footprint of a similar reptile long ago, traces of which have now disappeared!

In the Bog Meadows the sandstones are not so clearly evident on the surface except for the exposure in the low mound at the car-park of St. Gall's G.A.C. next to Milltown Cemetery. It was formerly much deeper and steeper as shown in the photograph below taken by the Northern Ireland Geological Survey in 1959 when it was used as a sand quarry but it is now largely obscured by the concrete retaining wall of the carpark. This red and yellow coloured outcrop consisted of layers of sandstone with intervening bands of mudstone formed mostly from desert dust winnowed by the constant winds that blew across the desert floor. Some of the layering or laminations seen in the sandstone is typical of layering seen in modern riverbeds or lakes and the presence of thin seams of mudstone indicate that these bodies of water occasionally dried out. Some of the individual grains here are typical of sand grains weathered by the wind. Occasionally when the shallow lakes evaporated coarser sand would cover the mudstones and infill any cracks as the mudstones dried up under the desert sun.

(Sherwood Sandstone Group)
Bunter Sandstone outcrop at the top of Rockdale Street

Red and yellow sandstone at Milltown (1959) Source: Geological Survey of Northern Ireland. Note the holes in the face of the sandstone on which the sandmartins built their nests.

Dolerite dyke at Milltown now covered by concrete retaining wall at St. Gall's GAC car park.

The colour of these sandstones and mudstones ranges from yellow to orange to red. These colours are derived from iron-oxides which are precipitated on to the sand and finer particles by the high temperatures experienced in a desert environment after moisture was evaporated off their minute surfaces. In much more recent geological times underground volcanic activity caused molten lava to rise through the layers of sandstone in vertical shafts or fissures occasionally several metres wide which split apart the sediments on the surface. In its passage the molten lava baked the sand and the mud so that they altered in colour and in texture becoming brittle and partially black. The molten lava eventually cooled into a hard black rock called dolerite and the small exposure of dolerite in the photograph forms a feature called a dyke. On both sides of the dyke can be seen the baked and fragmented sandstone and mudstone which was affected by the extreme heat.

9

CHAPTER 2
Glacial Events

The events that were mainly responsible for the present landscape of the Bog Meadows commenced during the Quaternary Period, which began some two million years BP and eventually waned 15,000 years BP (Before Present). The Quaternary Period is noted for the number of episodes or glaciations during which the earth experienced severe cold conditions that led to the formation of ice-sheets which covered a large part of the Northern Hemisphere. The conditions are similar to that which today covers most of Greenland to the depth of several hundred metres. These glacial events were separated by long inter-glacial periods lasting thousands of years during which the ice melted or retreated to higher ground allowing plants and animals to return. In the Lagan valley there is only evidence of the most recent glaciation that ended 15,000 years ago as each new advance of the ice has removed the evidence of the previous glaciation. At the peak of the last glaciation an ice -sheet enveloped the whole area of the Lagan valley and the surrounding hills forming a dome over the Lough Neagh basin and covering the South Antrim Hills with an axis running N.E to S.W. From this glacial mass ice descended to the lower ground moving in a southerly direction across the valley of the Lagan. This vast body of ice brought with it large quantities of local bedrock, sand and silt that was eroded from the land surface over which it passed. This material was held within and at the base of the ice sheet as long as the cold climate prevailed.

After many thousands of years elapsed, the climate ameliorated and gradually the ice mass melted releasing large thicknesses of boulders, gravel, sand and clay to cover the ground underneath. This material called glacial till blanketed the pre-glacial landscape, filling depressions including the deepest valleys and changing the shape of the topography in the vicinity of the Bog Meadows. The deep gorge which had previously existed on the western side of the Lagan Valley was buried under 60 metres of till largely derived from the bedrock. Red clay called Keuper Marl subsumed under the term 'Mercia Mudstone Group' is one of the main rock types at the base of the South

Section through Glacial Till along Ballymurphy River in Milltown Glen

Antrim Hills and is exposed on the ground west of the Bog Meadows and makes up the main matrix of the till.

As clay is plastic and easily moulded it lies as a thick sheet across the Bog Meadows with an occasional mound protruding above the surface. Lumps of flint and limestone occur within the glacial till indicating the northerly source of the ice movement. As a result of the decay of the ice-sheet 15,000 years ago large volumes of melt water were released which became impounded behind a wall of the ice mass as it retreated northwards towards the Irish Sea. This impounded lake deepened as melt water from localised ice pockets and rivers entered this lake referred to as Lake Lagan. (Fig 2.1).

Large amounts of sediment were deposited within this lake creating a long, low ridge of sand, gravel and clay that extended outwards from the centre of the lake which today forms the ridge of high ground along the Malone Road. This ridge lies on top of the basal clays and acts as a natural boundary to the Bog Meadows on the eastern side. Eventually the ice wall that impounded the glacial lake retreated northwards to release the waters into the direction of the Irish Sea. It left behind a landscape very different to that which had existed in pre-glacial times.

The Bog Meadows assumed much of its present form as a result of these glacial events. A low-lying area emerged, formed out of glacial clay hemmed

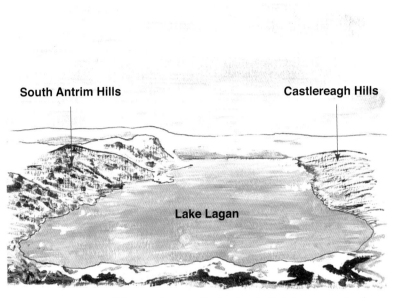

Fig. 2.1 *An impression of the scene in the late Ice Age showing Lake Lagan covering the Lagan valley. It is hemmed in by the retreating ice sheet to the north and the surrounding hills as shown.*

Fig 2.2 *The woolly mammoth, musk-ox and the wolf lived in the tundra conditions that prevailed in the Lagan valley during the interglacial that preceded the last glacial maximum 50,000 years ago. The mammoth and the musk-oxen did not survive the long glaciation which followed and became extinct in Ireland. Illustration based on an artist's impression in McKeever, P.J. A Story through Time. Landscapes from Stone, 1999. Geological Survey of Northern Ireland and the Geological Survey of Ireland.*

in by the Black Mountain to the west and the low ridge of glacial sands and gravels making up the Malone ridge to the east. This barren, cold and water covered landscape eventually changed as the climate ameliorated and hardy plants and animals migrated from the landmass of Britain and the Continent of Europe to which Ireland was still physically attached. In warmer periods between the cold episodes 50,000 years ago animals such as the woolly mammoth, the bear and musk oxen had adapted to the cold conditions at the edge of the retreating ice sheets and left evidence in the form of fossils that they grazed the tundra not far from the Lagan valley. (Fig 2.2)

They did not survive the long glacial period that began 25,000 BP and ended 13,000 BP. In the wake of the disappearing ice, tundra vegetation took hold to be replaced a thousand years later by a rich grassland landscape. In this habitat, a different group of animals prospered including the giant Irish deer and the reindeer. The giant Irish deer was a remarkable animal, majestic in size being over 2 metres in height with antlers stretching over two metres

from tip to tip. They must have roamed the hills and valleys around the Lagan valley as fossil remains have been found in the vicinity. They became extinct around 10,000 years ago after the climate deteriorated once again and ice masses began to form in the upland area.

Fig 2.3 *An artist's impression of the scene during the final glacial episode 10,000 years ago. It is dominated by the giant Irish deer that did not survive the harsh climatic conditions depicted as the grassland in which it had once flourished was replaced by tundra vegetation.*

CHAPTER 3
Post-Glacial Period

In post-glacial times the level of the waters in Belfast Lough rose as the meltwater released from the declining ice-sheets increased the volume of the nearby seas. Gradually these estuarine waters encroached upon the lowlying land at the confluence of the Lagan and the Blackstaff and penetrated farther inland turning the floodplain of the Blackstaff into an extension of the estuary of Belfast Lough. Only the Malone Ridge remained as a finger of glacial clays and sands jutting into these estuarine waters. The maximum extent of this inland lake is marked by the ancient shoreline depicted on Emrys Jones' map of the lower Lagan as coincident with the 25' contour line (Fig 3.1).

Over several thousand years these waters ebbed and flowed with the tides creating a shallow water environment for a range of freshwater and saltwater plants and marine life that adapted to the constantly changing conditions in this transitional area.

Over time layers of alluvium originating from the Blackstaff and its tributaries as well as the marine sediments covered the glacial till on the floodplain of the river as the estuarine waters penetrated farther inland. These marine sediments consisting of blue-grey clay, referred to locally as 'sleech', filled up all the depressions in the floor of the estuary and the Blackstaff river basin which vary in depth from seven metres near the Broadway underpass to twelve metres at Victoria Square in the city centre. Within these clays are the remains of numerous plants and shellfish which survived the harsh environment of these brackish waters. Reverend W.Smyth of St.John's Parish on the Falls Road recalled in 1954 how on the building of the parochial house on the slopes leading down to the Bog Meadows workmen unearthed beds of fossil oysters. Eventually, the oscillations of the level of the seas in relation to the land stabilised around 5,000 years ago that resulted in the retreat of the estuarine waters to a new shoreline roughly coincident with the present sea level. As a consequence the lower reaches of the Blackstaff were extended to a new confluence with the Lagan. The river meandered aimlessly across

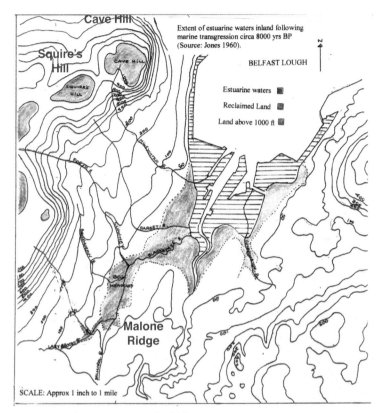

Fig. 3.1 *Extent of Estuarine Waters inland following marine transgression circa 8000 years B.P. (Source: Jones 1960).*

a flat area barely above sea-level and regularly covered with tidal waters when conditions allowed producing a landscape of shallows with occasional mudbanks exposed above the changing water levels. These tidal waters reached up to a point marked as the lowest convenient crossing point of the river and a suitable place for a bridge where the present Boyne Bridge is sited. From the upper reaches of the river system, the tributaries of the Blackstaff carried down large volumes of water especially in winter to pour across the mudbanks and shallows before they were checked by the presence of the tidal waters from Belfast Lough.

At first the climate in the post-glacial period was similar to that of the Tundra of the Arctic and the plants and animals that lived were indicative of these cold conditions. Plants of the open tundra such as juniper and other low growing shrubs eventually gave way as the climate grew warmer to birch woods and then to dense forests of hazel, oak and elm with pinewoods on the hilltops. Layers of peat that formed in the forest clearings are found today under the Bog Meadows at a depth of 5 metres. In one such layer animals remains including red deer were discovered when workmen were digging foundations for a reservoir at the lower end of Broadway in 1902.

'Sleech'

basal
sandstone

Illustration showing the excavation through 12 metres at 'Sleech' at Victoria Square, Belfast, 2005

CHAPTER 4
The River System

As the climate grew warmer at the end of the Ice Age springs began to flow from under the limestone where it outcrops along the foot of the escarpment that stretches from Hannastown to the Cave Hill.. This spring line is marked by a series of small rivulets that emerge where the limestone rests on top of an impermeable layer of clay and are recognised on the O.S. map with the letters spr. These small ribbons of water grew in size as they flowed downhill coalescing with other streams until they formed the network of rivers that entered the Bog Meadows. The Blackstaff previously called the Black Water is the main river and one might think its name was derived from its colour. Its name, however, is based not on the colour of the water but on the colour of the staves which were placed across the channel as a makeshift bridge in the past and which over time turned black in the water-logged ground. These staves or planks were made of oak, called 'bior' in Gaelic, the plural of which is 'beara'. The combination of the Gaelic words for 'river' and 'staves' produces Abhainn Bheara , which comes down to us as Owenvarragh, the ancient name of the river and a local street name today. (McKay, 1999). The Forth River which is the main tributary commences high up on the eastern side of Divis Mountain and is fed by several springs as it flows downhill along a steep channel which increased the erosive power of this river. The effect of increased power is evident in the steep sided valley along its course as it cuts a deep channel from Ballysillan to Beechmount. The names of rivers often reveal something about the area through which they flow or some feature along its course. The Forth River when it reaches the lower ground at Beechmount is renamed the Clowney. The Clowney once joined the Blackstaff at the back of Celtic Park before road changes brought about the diversion and culverting of the lower reaches of the river. The name 'Forth' is derived from one of the 'forts' or raths that existed on the slopes leading up to Divis Mountain. The lower stretch of the river referred to as the 'Clowney' flowed gently across undulating land around present day Beechmount. The name is derived from the Gaelic word 'cluain' meaning a

meadow. The meadow would have been on both sides of the river rising up to the higher ground towards the Springfield and Whiterock Roads. The other tributaries of the Blackstaff include some that are unnamed and others that have acquired modern names such as 'Woodlands' and 'Ladybrook'. The Woodlands River is a continuation of the Ladybrook River and is now culverted along its course. One river which is not named on the maps of the area is known locally as the Ballymurphy River the name of the townland area through which it flows on its way to join the Blackstaff. This river goes under the Falls Road next to Maguire's garage, along the boundary of the cemetery and through Milltown to link up with the Blackstaff following a series of channel adjustments that divert it under the M1 motorway. Another tributary of the Blackstaff which is unnamed on the O.S. map flows under the Falls Road and emerges for a short distance near Sinclair's Garage. It is named in this text as the Andersonstown River.

A remnant of the ancient boundary between Ballydownfine and Ballymoney represented by a stretch of the Andersonstown River.

The tributaries from the western side of the Bog Meadows flow down the steep slope of the escarpment and carry a large volume of water towards the lower ground below. In winter this discharge was augmented with seasonally high rainfall that turned each river and stream into a torrent. When the discharge was checked on reaching the main channel of the Blackstaff the riverbanks were unable to contain the sudden increases in the volume of water

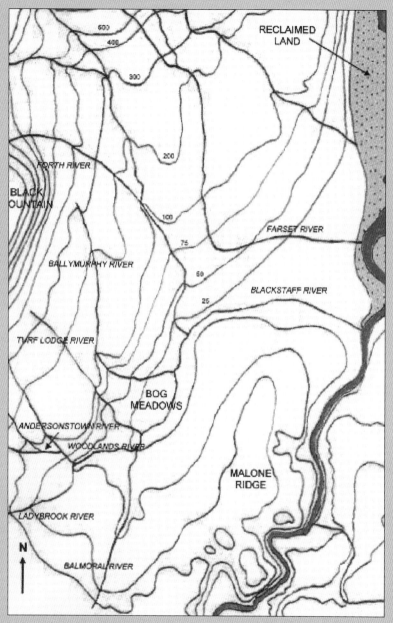

Fig. 4.1 *BLACKSTAFF RIVER SYSTEM SOURCE: JONES, E.. A Social Geography of Belfast. 1960. Oxford University Press. (Height in feet about sea level)*

and spilled over them. Most of the Bog Meadows was then inundated with the floodwaters extending outwards towards the Falls Road and Lisburn Road. The extent of the floodwaters was often affected by the state of the tides in Belfast Lough that held back the flow of the Lagan river into the estuary and the consequent effect on the Blackstaff as a tributary of the Lagan.

In addition to the floodwaters brought down from the foot of the escarpment, the tributaries of the Blackstaff carried heavy loads of silt eroded from the mantle of glacial debris that covered the lower slopes. The regular inundation of the floodplain of the Blackstaff caused the deposition of a thin veneer of silt every time the river broke its banks. The build up of sediment over the years resulted in a thick layer of alluvium covering the Bog Meadows which thinned out away from the banks of the river on either side. (Fig 4.2)

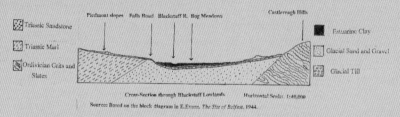

Fig. 4.2 *Cross-Section through Blackstaff Lowlands. Horizontal Scale 1:1500,000. Source: Based on the block diagram in E Evans, The Site of Belfast, 1944.*

CHAPTER 5
Early History

The earliest inhabitants of Ireland arrived some 9,000 years ago during a period known as the Mesolithic or Middle Stone Age. They first settled along the riverbanks of the Lower Bann River and the Antrim coast. Their settlements were in close proximity to outcrops of chalk under the basalt cover of the Antrim plateau. Within the chalk were nodules of flint from which they shaped implements such as blades, scrapers and arrowheads. They were hunters and gatherers, hunting red deer and wild boar as well as game birds. The lakes, rivers and coastal waters provided an ample supply of fish including shellfish.

Small family hunting groups must have ventured across the higher slopes of the Antrim plateau that was heavily forested. Others engaged in a form of trade by carrying flint nodules and finished flint tools to other places for other groups in the north of Ireland. They approached the Lagan valley by means of the low cols at Tornaroy and Ligoniel at a height of 200 metres above sea level. Before them lay a forest covered landscape stretching as far as the eye could see with the mountains of Mourne, and Slieve Gullion in the distance to the south. To the north was a similar scene with the forest enveloping the lowlands of the Lagan and the Blackstaff. (Fig 5.1)

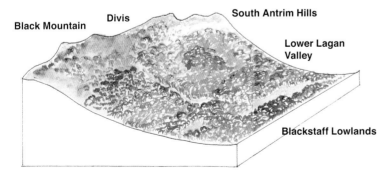

Fig. 5.1 *An artist's impression of the South Antrim Hills and lower slopes during the Mesolithic period when it was covered with a thick deciduous forest on the edge of which Mesolithic hunters made their camps.*

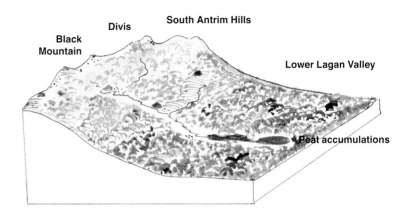

Fig 5.2 *A scene from the Neolithic Age showing the Black Mountain area and hill slopes where Neolithic farmers had cleared the upper slopes for cultivation. Here is where burial mounds and stone pillars are to be found today.*

The rivers and surrounding forest offered a rich resource for those small family groups who wished to remain in the area but acted as a formidable obstacle to those wishing to cross from one side of the Lagan valley to the other. Within the forest they could hunt for deer and wild boar and along the edges of Belfast Lough they could collect cockles and clams, conscious of the bears and wolves that roamed among the thickets of hazel, willow and alder. No evidence exists of their habitations around the Blackstaff River but several clues remain that they lived and hunted in close proximity. Those clues consist of numerous flint blades, points and other implements that have been found in the region that have been dated to this prehistoric period.

Around 6,000 years ago in a period called the Neolithic or New Stone age, family groups migrated to the north of Ireland over the Irish Sea from Britain with domestic animals such as cattle, pigs and sheep. They began to clear the forest which had been untouched for thousands of years with heavier implements. Within these forest clearings animals could be grazed and crops planted. They concentrated their farming activities on the higher ground of the South Antrim hills where the decomposed basalt gave a friable soil. Burial sites, cairns, and standing stoned testify to their presence. The distinctive burnished pottery of this period as well as flint implements has turned up at Malone and Dunmurry along the ancient trackway from Tornaroy to the Giant's Ring skirting the Blackstaff and avoiding the need to cross it at some point. (Fig 5.2)

In addition to the movement of people and animals along tracks between Antrim and Down, there was also a movement of goods in the form of polished axe heads made from a rare exceptionally hard rock called porcellanite. These axe heads have been found in different parts of Ireland and Britain indicating that trade was very much a feature of this society. A large hoard of such tools was found at Ormeau on the banks of the Lagan and individual axe heads found in the Malone area.

Whilst the Blackstaff River hindered movement across valley, the river provided food in form of salmon and other fish as well as edible plants such as watercress. In the nearby forest on both banks of the river there were game birds to be hunted such as wild pigeon and woodcock, plants and berries to eat.

The arrival of Celtic peoples around 500 BC came at a time when the climate was changing, becoming increasingly colder and wetter. The higher parts of the mountain and hills were gradually abandoned and settlement was confined to the lower slopes. Technology was also changing as these migrants brought with them tools and weapons made of iron, changes that were to have a dramatic effect on the landscape as heavy axes reduced the forest cover. In addition the increased number of grazing animals made it necessary to cut down trees to provide pasture. On the hilltops blanket bog, which had increased its extent since the Bronze Age, replaced the woodland and the summits became unattractive for settlement. (Fig 5.3)

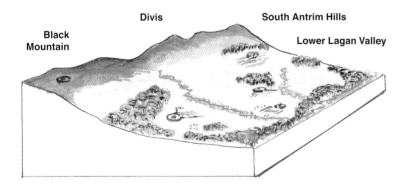

Fig 5.3 An artist's impression of the landscape changes that took place during the latter half of the last millennium BC when as a result of the expansion of grazing areas, the hill tops were cleared of trees and blanket bog increased.

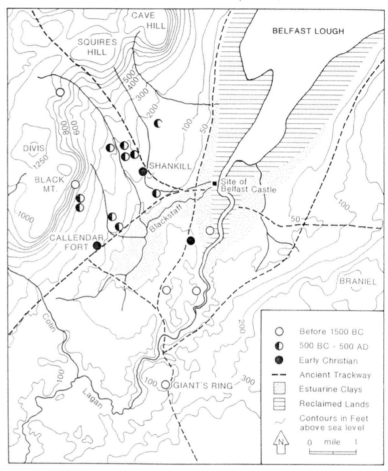

ANCIENT TRACKWAYS OF LAGAN VALLEY
(modified after Evans, 1944)

Fig. 5.4 Distribution of Early Christian Raths on the slopes of the South Antrim Hills.

The coming of Christianity brought with it an increase in population that in turn led to an expansion of farming and a further reduction in the forest cover. More and more habitations were constructed in individual farmsteads called raths or ringforts although the latter term implies a defensive purpose that few seem to have possessed. Each farmstead had small fields adjoining it with patches of woodland separated by open pastures. A form

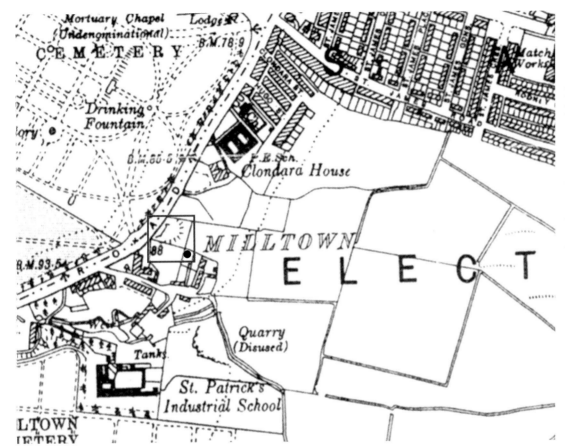

Fig. 5.5 *Remains of a rath which has been bisected by the new alignment of the Falls Road in the mid 19th century. 12" Map of Belfast, 1909.*

It is certain that others existed on these lower slopes below the Black Mountain but have been buried under housing estates and other developments in the name of progress. One such rath was known as Callender's Fort and was identified as such on the early O.S. maps of the area but now lies buried under the detached houses on the Glen Road opposite Arizona Street. It was in the townland of Ballydownfine and may well be the 'white fort' which the name signifies. The middle term of the name, Ir. dun suggests a swelling or residence of an important person as the term is often associated with a king's residence. The position of the rath along the bank of the 'Gully' River and near the arterial route of the Falls Road provides further proof that this was an important site. In addition, there is some evidence to suggest that a crannog was built in the lowlying ground referred to in modern times as Lake Glen. The physical evidence is the existence of lowlying ground close to the ringfort that was later called Lake Glen. In this hollow a mound of earth, clay and stones was built and on the platform above a dwelling was constructed to provide shelter in case of danger. Around the crannog water from the nearby river was diverted to afford some limited form of obstacle to any intruder. Map informationn is based on Lindquist's map of 1770 in which the site is represented by a symbol for a church and named 'Crannoge' (Fig 5.6, P20) (see Chapter 6).

of transhumance was practised whereby cattle were herded to the hilltops in summer time to graze the upper meadows and brought down in the autumn before the winter set in again. (Fig 5.4)

Nearly twenty of these raths have been recorded from O.S. maps between Black Mountain and Cave Hill. Such was their number at one time that the river that flows in between them is called the Forth (Fort) River as described in Chapter 4. Overlooking the Bog Meadows were several raths mostly between the 150m and 275m contours. One of them became known as Piper's Hill and remained as a low mound within the grounds of MacRory Park until it as demolished when the park was turned into a military base during the 1970s. The remains of another rath lay closer to the Bog Meadows on a site now occupied by Millcourt Residential Homes (5.5).

These ringforts and surrounding pastures increased in number during the Early Christian period and expanded further into the woodland. Their expansion created the need for territorial boundaries as petty chieftains exerted local control over a number of farmsteads and their occupants. These boundaries created the townlands that persist today in the local place names

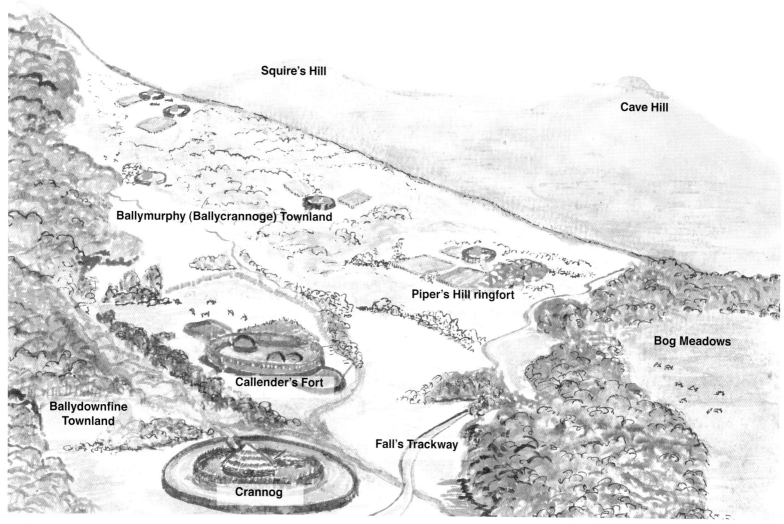

Squire's Hill

Cave Hill

Ballymurphy (Ballycrannoge) Townland

Piper's Hill ringfort

Bog Meadows

Callender's Fort

Ballydownfine Townland

Fall's Trackway

Crannog

and which are still part of the administrative structure of local government. The boundaries of the townlands that make up the Blackstaff lowlands conform to the existing physical features usually the rivers and small streams that form part of the natural drainage system. The boundaries also cut across the main lines of communications in the region running counter to the direction of the ancient tracks along the Falls Road and Malone Ridge and continuing up slope to the top of Black Hill and Black Mountain.

The layout of the townlands show that the Blackstaff River and its tributaries acted as an important dividing line between eight of the townlands in the lower Lagan Valley. Thus the townlands of Ballydownfine and Ballymurphy were separated by a river that had its origins above The Allens or The Dun Ravine, better known as 'The Gully', and joined the Blackstaff near the present sewage works on Stockman's Lane. Between Ballydownfine and Ballymoney flowed a river that is now culverted below Andersonstown and only a remnant of it can be seen near Sinclair's garage on the Falls Road. The Forth River acted as a boundary between Ballymagarry and Edenderry.

The names of these townlands have been anglicised in their spelling from their Gaelic origins that often obscures their true meaning. Ballygammon, Ir. Baile Gamhna, 'townland of the calf': Ballydownfine, Ir. Baile Dun Fionn, 'townland of the white fort': Ballymurphy, Ir. Baile Ui Mhurchu, 'townland of (the descendants of) O Murchu': Ballymagarry, Ir. Baile an Garrai, 'McGarry's Town': Edenderry, Ir. Eadan Doire, 'hillface of oaks': Malone, Ir. Maigh Luain, 'Luan's Plain' or 'plain of the lambs': and Ballyfinaghy, Ir. Baine an Fhionnachaidh, 'townland of the white field'. Unfortunately those linked with the lower reaches of the Blackstaff have gone out of use and their meanings are obscure. (Ui Fhlannagain, D. 1982)

A man-made ditch that acted as the ancient boundary between the townlands of Ballymoney and Ballydownfine on the slopes of the Black Mountain

Boundary between the townlands of Ballygammon and Ballymoney in the form of the Woodlands River now buried under the roundabout at Stockman's Lane.

CHAPTER 6
Early Ecclesiastical Sites

Despite the traditional belief that St. Patrick spent some considerable time in the north-east of Ireland preaching the new gospel of Christianity, there is a dearth of foundations around Belfast that testify to his influence and missionary zeal. One foundation of some importance was the medieval parish church of Shankhill Ir. sean chill 'old church', now occupied by the present Church of Ireland church of St. Matthew. Friar's Bush on the Malone ridge was another place of some significance. It appears to have been a monastic settlement and is named as Kilpatrick Ir. cill phadraig, 'Patrick's church' in Dr.Reeve's Ecclesiastical History. In later times a Crown Grant to the Marquis of Donegall in 1828 refers to the site as Ballybragher, Ir. Baile na mBragher, 'townland of the friars'. It fell into decay long before this but continued to be used by Catholics as burial ground until 1828. There is a reference in O'Laverty to the tradition of celebrating Sunday mass in the open air at this site in the middle of the 18th century.

To reach Friar's Bush from the townlands of Ballymurphy or Ballydownfine, people would have had to cross the lower reaches of the Blackstaff at the bridge near the present Boyne Bridge or take the alternative cross valley route along Stockman's Lane. A more convenient journey could be made directly across the Bog Meadows during dry weather by crossing the Blackstaff before its junction with the Clowney River. This fording point would allow the travellers to head towards the lower slopes of the Malone Ridge roughly following the line of Blackstaff Lane (Donegall Road). This fording point is later marked on the early editions of the O.S. maps of the area that supports the view that this ford was once part of an important cross- valley route linking the trackway along the present Giant's Foot and St. James's Park to Blackstaff Lane and beyond. (Fig 6.1)

Fig 6.1 *Map redrawn from the O.S. map of County Antrim, Sheet 60, 1857 showing the ford over the Blackstaff River before its junction with the Clowney River linking the Falls with the Malone Ridge. Scale: 1:10,640*

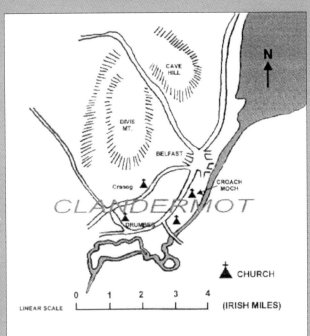

Fig. 6.2 *Reproduction of 'A map of County Antrim', reduced and drawn from Mr Lendrick's map by W.A. Williamson, 1807. Scale: 3 Irish Miles to an inch. PRONI [T/1129/234]. It shows the location of Callender's Fort referred to as 'cranog' confirming the link with a crannog in the vicinity.*

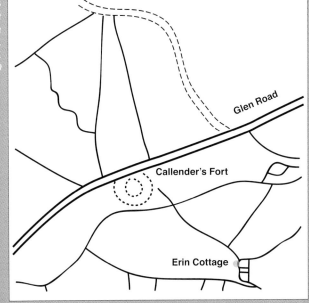

Fig 6.3 *Callender's Fort as depicted on O.S. Sheet 60. Antrim 1857. Scale:1:10,560*

Fig 6.4   *Artist's impression of the ruins of the church at Callender's fort referred to as 'Cranog'. The continued use of the site as a place to bury the dead is testified by the reports of a large quantity of bones that were unearthed when the Glen Road was being laid down (O'Byrne, 1946).*

There are a few foundations of lesser importance along the Falls trackway as evidenced in the townland names of Killeaton and Kilmakee. Near Suffolk village there was a church site called Kilwee, Ir. cill buidhe 'the yellow church' or cill uaidh 'the church of the graveyard'. Its location was placed on the west bank of the Colin River but no physical evidence remains of this church. It had been used as a burial place in the late 18th and early 19th centuries according to O'Byrne. Overlooking the Bog Meadows was another ecclesiastical foundation built on top of a raised mound that may have been an abandoned rath or one that had been set aside by the local chieftain as a place of worship. It was not unusual for such foundations to use earlier structures such as farmsteads on which to build along with their defensive banks and ditches. This site is identified on Linquist's map of 1780 as a church site with a church symbol placed on the side of the Falls trackway with the name Cranog. This suggests that the name is associated with the presence at some time in the past with a nearby crannog as mentioned in the previous chapter. When it fell into disuse as a church the grounds around it continued to be used as a burial ground similar to Friar's Bush. That may have caused its name to change from crannoge to cealluir or ceallurach, Ir. ' Burial ground' and further changed to Callender, hence Callender's Fort. In an article written for the Ulster Journal of Archaeology (1903) Dr Reeves states that Callender's Fort was built on *'a slight elevation. On this site was a chapel, the walls of which were remembered to have been standing; and the font belonging to which was in the possession of the person who held the ground. The spot is now covered with a mantle of grass, but the foundations of the building can be distinctly traced, measuring about 114 feet by 40 feet. The surrounding ground is stated to have been occupied by a burying ground. (Fig 6.2, 6.3, 6.4).*

CHAPTER 7

Viking Attacks in the Lagan valley

The few early Christian churches in the Lagan valley were at risk of attack from Viking raiders who swept along the coastline of Ireland at the end of the eighth century. They penetrated up the various rivers in search of monastic sites for it was such places of learning that offered the best spoils. Coastal monastic sites were especially vulnerable and the records recall constant attacks on Bangor Abbey in 823 and Nendrum at the head of Strangford Lough. It is more than likely that the Norsemen would have sailed up the estuary of Belfast referred to then as Loch Lao and viewed the terrain from the waters of the lough.

The Lagan river gave access to the lower Lagan valley and the possibility of progressing further west into the forests between the Lagan and Lough Neagh (Loch nEathach). A Viking fleet had managed to enter Lough Neagh by navigating a passage down the River Bann (An Bhanna). It is fair to assume that longships or their smaller counterparts which had only a beam of 2.8 metres could have penetrated inland along the Lagan. However the only continuous stretch of navigable water ends at Stranmillis the highest point of tidal waters. Beyond that there are several obstacles in the way of waterfalls and rapids. Another line of approach by the Vikings would have been to send small groups of warriors a short distant inland from the mouth of the Blackstaff in their smaller crafts particularly when the river was in flood, to reconnoitre the more open region between the Malone ridge and the escarpment of the South Antrim Hills. They could beach their ships large or small on the mudflats of the river mouths and march inland along the tracks that radiated west and north from the ford at the mouth of the Farset river.

There is no reference to any such incursions along the Lagan or in the vicinity of the Blackstaff but such was the strength and duration of Viking raids in the early part of the tenth century that it is conceivable that the native Irish living in isolated communities throughout the Lagan valley lived in fear of attack Bardon (2005). It was in this period that monks took refuge in their tall tapered round towers built of stone. The nearest one to the Bog Meadows lies in the shadow of the old church site at Drumbo in Co, Down. All that remains is the stump of the tower but one can imagine the view that an observer from the top would have as he looked northward towards the Lagan estuary. Perhaps he gave warning of the approach of the Norsemen advancing on the church along the Malone ridge or advancing across the ford on the Lagan at Ballylesson from the Falls direction.

CHAPTER 8
The Coming of the Normans

The advance into Ulster by the Normans led by John de Courcy in 1177 heralded in a new era in which Norman knights established control over east Ulster. In south Antrim and east Down earthen mottes and stone castles were thrown up to form a network holding the conquered lands in subjection and allowing access to the sea. Several of these mottes were built in the vicinity of the Bog Meadows which as before presented a natural barrier to east-west communications in the lower Lagan valley. A large motte was built on a hill in Dunmurry next to an Early Christian rath. Between the mouth of the Farset river and the Blackstaff the Normans constructed a castle which was attacked on several occasions by the local Irish chieftains. Other mottes which were constructed included a motte at Castle Robin west of Hannastown and at Shaw's bridge guarding the passage over the Lagan. These outposts acted as sentinels providing early warning of imminent attack from raiders approaching from the west. They remained within visibility of each other for safety, the castle at Le Ford (Belfast)was within sight of Dunmurry motte across the wetlands of the Bog Meadows and it in turn could be seen from Castle Robin. Movement between these Norman defensive sites was often hazardous. To reach Dunmurry motte from Le Ford the Blackstaff had to be crossed at its lowest bridging point at the present Sandy Row. To reach it via Tough na Fall (the Falls) meant a longer journey across the numerous tributaries of the Blackstaff. It would not have been an unusual sight to witness parties of French –speaking mailed horsemen trying to negotiate a way across the Clowney, Ballymurphy, and Colin rivers as they set out to reach their comrades at the motte of Dunmurry. Given the often fractious relationships between the different groups of Norman knights and their kinsmen, Gaelic chieftains and their followers, landed freemen and their villiens, it is probable that numerous skirmishes occurred when advantage was sought or opportunities arose to bring disagreements into open conflict. The fording points across the tributaries of the Blackstaff would have been ideal places to lie in wait for approaching parties of horsemen and their wagons. It is easy to imagine confrontations at these places between the native Irish, the Norman overlords and their allies which would have deterred any attempt to encourage large-scale settlement in the Lagan valley.

The Normans were more inclined towards *control and consolidation than conquest and colinisation. (Bardon, 1982)* They remained confined to their mottes and stone castles with few settlers outside their defensive sites. They were content to allow the native Irish to continue with their way of life, to herd their cattle according to custom, to farm their enclosed fields for cereals such as oats and to remain in their homesteads or raths which were scattered across the lower slopes of the South Antrim Hills.

Some native Irish were substantial farmers but most were villiens or freemen who held small holdings in return for service to the local Norman baron. Much of the rents was paid in corn. Landholders could increase their income by charging for the use of their corn-mills. One of these was unearthed at the side of the Forth River in Beechmount. The Bog Meadows would have been a substantial source of food for the inhabitants of the raths that existed at that time, providing them with wildfowl, nuts, wild fruits, fungi, fish and edible water plants such as watercress. Its resources would have been shared between the local people in accordance with Gaelic custom of the time although fishing rights along the Blackstaff River itself may have belonged to the local Norman overlord.

This relationship between ruling classes and the governed remained more or less intact until the commencement of the Elizabethan wars in 1558 and the destruction of the Gaelic order and the wholesale change of authority and ownership of the territory of Clandeboye in which the Bog Meadows and surrounding lands were located.

CHAPTER 9
'Newtown Chichester'

Clandeboye was the territory ruled by Clann Aodha Buidhe, a sect of the O'Neill dynasty. It was divided by the river Lagan into Lower and Upper Clandeboye. Lower Clandeboye covered most of South Antrim including the Bog Meadows, the Falls and the surrounding hillslopes across to and including the Malone ridge.

Conn O'Neill was the last Gaelic chieftain to rule Clandeboye. Through trickery, imprisonment and threats to his life, he lost most of his lands to two Scottish adventurers, Hamilton and Montgomery. Among the many who subsequently benefited from the eventual redistribution of these vast acreages was Arthur Chichester. He was given the small settlement of Belfast and adjoining lands as well as large tracts elsewhere in Ulster. One of his first actions was to protect the town of Belfast by building a castle to guard the ford across the Lagan which linked Lower Clandeboye on the Antrim side of the Lagan River with the lands of Upper Clandeboye on the County Down side. This castle was also sited to keep watch on the ford over the Blackstaff at the lowest crossing point somewhere in the vicinity of the present Boyne bridge.

Chichester planned to exploit these properties by renting them out on favourable terms to those who had assisted him during the Nine Years war against Hugh O'Neill of Tyrone. First the lands were surveyed and were allocated in due course to those of his former lieutenants and then later to those immigrants from Scotland and England who undertook to farm the lands they received and to look after them according to strict conditions.

Conn O'Neill had briefly supported Hugh O'Neill in his war against the English crown. The native Irish families in Lower Clandeboye suffered as a consequence. They were driven out and had their lands confiscated. Many retreated to the higher ground that was less attractive to the new arrivals and eventually became undertenant farmers of various landlords or leaseholders. The latter were content to receive some return on these more isolated properties on the exposed upper slopes of the South Antrim Hills.

The changes to ownership and authority over these lands had been dramatic. In the space of twenty to thirty years the old Gaelic order and way of life was swept aside and the customs, language and religion of the planters held sway over the whole of the Lagan Valley.

The replacement of a Gaelic lordship economy by a market-style economy had a major impact on both the landscape and ways of living. The land was regarded as an asset that had to be turned into a profitable commodity. As an asset its extent had to be measured and mapped. Boundaries which may have been ill-defined in the past had to be more carefully delineated and managed especially when it was being leased in large units. From the beginning of the seventeenth century onwards there was an increase in the laws governing land ownership and the making of estate maps. One such estate map was that drawn up by James Crow on behalf of the Earl of Donegall's Estates in the Lagan valley and elsewhere from 1770-1776. (Fig.9.1)

TOWN OF BELFAST

Note: Modern names in
brackets (eg. Ladybrook)
Scale 1 : 2500 approx

River Lagan

Cromac Wood

Townland of
BALLYMURPHY

DEMESNE
LANDS

Blackwater
(Blackstaff)

MALONE ROAD

Milltown Village

LOWER MALONE

Townland of
Ballydownfine

(Woodlands River)

(Ladybrook River)

Townland of
Ballymoney

UPPER MALONE

Fig.9.1 *THE BLACKSTAFF WETLANDS AND MALONE,
1770: based on plans of the Earl of Donegall's Estates, surveyed
by James Crow. 1776-1770 (PRONI D/835/1/3/18-21)*

It covered the lands in the area of the Bog Meadows
and showed the acreages leased out to different
tenants It used the old townland boundaries which
are clearly defined, evidence of the need to ensure a
smooth transition from one form of landholding to
another.

Some of the leaseholders can be identified by
matching their acreages to the name of the leaseholder
from the Hearth Money Rolls for the different
townlands. One such leaseholder was James Saurin
who had a lease of 52 acres 4 perches in the townland
of Ballymurphy. Judging from the number of hearths
listed in the townland, he had few neighbours there
or in the adjoining townlands compared to the
townlands of Upper or Lower Malone. Along the Falls
Road a few individual houses had clustered together
to form the village of Anderson's Town. (Fig.9.2)

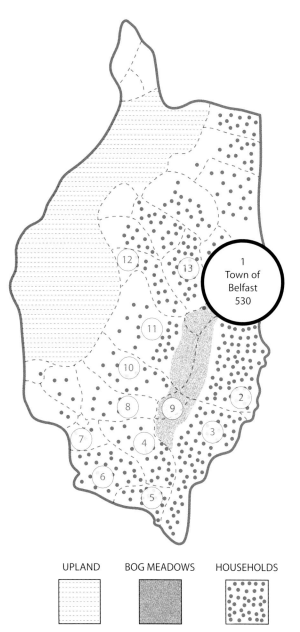

**Parishes of
Shankhill and
Drumbeg**

1. Town of Belfast
2. Malone lower
3. Malone Upper
4. Ballyfinaghy
5. Old Forge
6. Dunmurry (Pt)
7. Dunmurry (Pt)
8. Ballymoney
9. Ballygammon
10. Ballydownfine
11. Ballymurphy
12. Ballymagarry
13. Edenderry

UPLAND   BOG MEADOWS   HOUSEHOLDS

Fig.9.2. Distribution of hearths in the townlands around the Bog Meadows. Source: Robinson,T., Heads and Hearths. PRONI.

The general layout of the farms and other properties does not suggest any overall pattern except in the vicinity of the Blackstaff River where the boundaries of each lease run at right angles to the riverbank. This meant sharing the varying soil and drainage conditions encountered on the slopes leading down to the river. This pattern is more evident on the opposite side of the Blackstaff where the farms of the Malone ridge parallel each other as they reach down towards the river. They share in equal measure the changing soil and drainage conditions between the ridge top and the estuarine muds of the Bog Meadows. From the leases it can be deduced that the leaseholders were all tenant farmers before the expansion of Belfast transformed the area with its country lodges and 'gentlemen's places'. (Benn, 1880)

Elsewhere along the lower course of the Blackstaff the ancient townland names had long been abandoned and incorporated within the title of Townparks. This name in part, reflected the desire of the Third Earl of Donegall to create suitable 'pleasure grounds' in the vicinity of the town. Part of the south side of the lower Blackstaff was maintained as Cromac Wood. It was full of oak and elm and served as a deerpark for the Donegall family. The rest of Townparks was leased out to numerous tenants whose leases averaged three acres. (Fig. 9.3)

It is clear from the survey by James Crow that the physical landscape of the Blackstaff lowlands had changed irrevocably. The extensive woodlands which had once clothed the hillslopes of the Black Mountain and Divis ranges had been gradually cleared and irregular-shaped farms were laid out in place of the scattered homesteads and grazing areas centred around the individual raths. These farmsteads took advantage of elevated, south-facing and well-drained sites along the foothills to form the core of several of Belfast's early suburbs such as Springfield, Milltown, Anderson's Town and Suffolk. Several residences were set off from the road complete with their gate houses such as at Beechmount, and Willowbank.

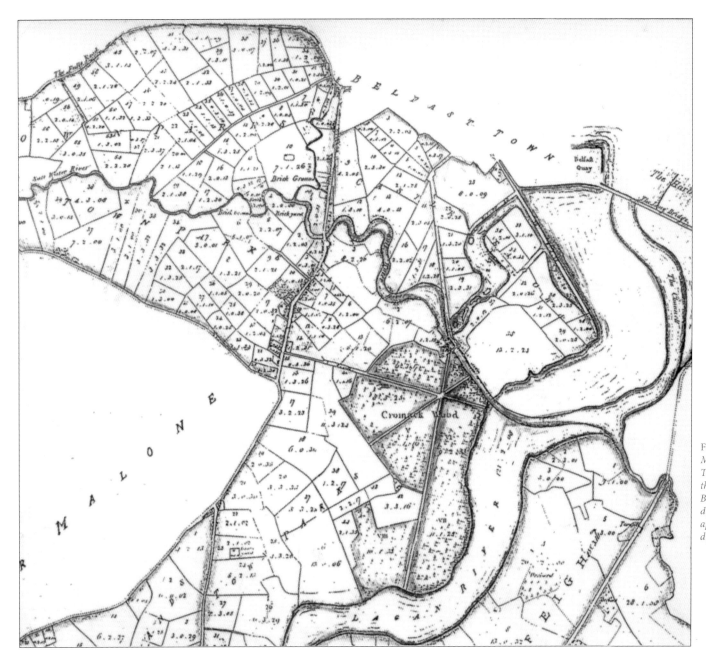

Fig. 9.3 *Donegall Estate Map 1770 includes Town Parks area along the lower reaches of the Blackstaff. It shows the different acreages apportioned to the different leaseholders.*

CHAPTER 10
Industrial Expansion along the Blackstaff (1750 –1850)

Industrial activity in the Blackstaff basin during the latter half of the 18th century was confined largely to the headwater streams of the Farset and Ballymurphy Rivers. Along both banks was to be found rubbing mills, bleachworks, bleachgreens and workers' housing. In the lower reaches of the Blackstaff at the point where the river was diverted eastwards by an artificial cut stood the paper mill of the Joy family. Henry Joy (1720-1789) had acquired a lease from the Earl of Donegall in May, 1767 for 1 acres 2 roods 30 perches to build a paper mill on the south bank of the Blackstaff. Power for the water wheel was supplied by tidal water flowing to the Lagan via the Blackstaff fed in part by the old abandoned portion of the river in addition to the volume of water coming down from the tributaries. In 1780 this water supply was considered inadequate, so Henry Joy took out an additional lease of 7 acres 2 roods of land to the north of the paper mill and excavated a large mill dam that incorporated the old abandoned stretch of the Blackstaff. (Muir, 2004). Fig 10.1.

It is evident from these maps that Belfast was a town of no great size but things began to change with the coming of the new century when financial difficulties of the Donegall family created the conditions for expansion. The Donegall family had been in possession of the town since the time that their ancestor Sir Arthur Chichester was granted the manor of Belfast and 52 townlands by James 1 in 1603. They were the authors of their own demise, the result of which meant that the town was no longer their private property. George Augustus, the second Marquess of Donegall found himself in a debtor's prison in 1795 and owed his release to the intervention of a moneylender by the name of Edward May. He then married Edward May's sister possibly one of the conditions of his release or more likely his desire to become a brother-in-law of the owner of a gambling house! He moved to Belfast in 1802 where he became involved in a number of schemes to help the town such as the building of the Fever Hospital in 1817 and the gas works in 1823. To ease his financial burdens, however, he renewed leases in the town on very favourable terms in return for substantial entry fines (Benn, 1823). Some of the most favourable terms were granted to Edward May who acquired long leases of parts of the Donegall property at low rents on the north side of the Blackstaff estuary. Most of the land leased was reclaimed slobland, land that was frequently inundated by the sea aided by winter floodwaters of the Blackstaff. Part of the estate was on land that had once formed part of the lower course of the Blackstaff before it was diverted directly to the Lagan at Cromac. This had been accomplished in the previous century by digging an artificial channel or 'cut'. The mud removed from this excavation was formed into a sea-bank that protected the inner part from incursions by tidal waters.

Fig.10.1 *Joy's papermill on the Blackstaff at Cromac .*

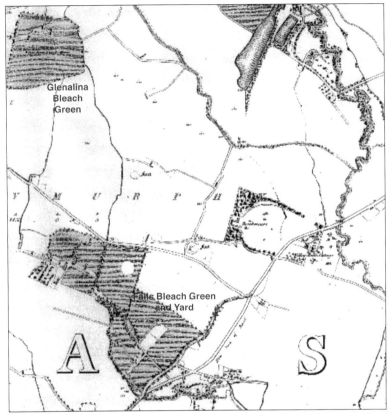

Milltown Village as seen from the Bog Meadows

Fig 10.5 *Falls and Glenalina Bleach Greens and Bleach Yards. O.S.Map, Co Antrim Sheet 60, 1834/35. Scale 1:10560*

spinning in 1828. Within a few years the linen spinning industry had become firmly established in Belfast. (Monaghan, 1942)

By the 1840s and 1850s the early industrial landscape of the western approaches to Belfast with its pattern of bleach works and associated small settlements such as Springfield was transformed by the erection of new large spinning mills located on green field sites down towards the town centre.

The main Falls Road spinning mills were located along the banks of the Farset downstream from the original mountain bleaching enterprises that were forced to consolidate into much bigger greens and associated works.

Such a bleach green with attendant works and outbuildings was laid out over what is now the Falls Park. Fig 10.5.

Technological change was also affecting the ways in which the linen cloth was finished. Beetling engines were introduced into the Lagan Valley as early as 1725. This new technology was utilised by all drapers by the turn of the 19th century. A row of heavy wooden beams was dropped onto the linen cloth that gave it a glossy sheen or lustre to linen garments such as hollands, buckrams and book-binding cloth. (Bardon 1982). The hammering of the wooden beams lasted a long time, perhaps two weeks to complete the process. The noise generated by the constant pounding was so loud that beetling mills were located away from habitations. Milltown Glen, a secluded and remote setting, was chosen as a site for such an operation. The mill was built on the banks of the Ballymurphy River using the power of the river to turn the waterwheel. The men who operated the machines lived close by in the cottages owned probably by the mill owners and several successive generations of the same family passed on the skills of the craft. The mill had three floors. On the ground floor would have been the beetling engines driven by an external water wheel. The upper floors were used to dry the beetled cloth. The building was converted in later times to an industrial school for boys. (See overleaf)

The ruins of the beetling mill at Milltown before demolition to make way for an extension of the garage above it.

The engine house that provided steam power to drive the machinery in the dye and print works at Milltown from the early years of the 19th century onwards

The remains of the cotton mill at Milltown specialising in the dyeing and printing of the fabrics. Later flax and hemp yarns were bleached

Pat Hughes, the 'Bog Meadow's Bachelor' (photo courtesy of the Andersonstown News.

The manager's office attached to the cotton mill in the early years of the Milltown operation. It was the residence of the Owen's family in more recent times who sold it to the D.O.E. in 1992 for use as a centre for the proposed developments in the Bog Meadows. It was vandalised soon afterwards and demolished.

This building functioned as a warehouse for the dye and print works. The gable end of the building was the home of Pat Hughes shown above, whose father raised cattle in the fields nearby. This building, including his home, was burned down in an arson attack in 2007.

CHAPTER 11

Industrial Expansion along the Blackstaff (1850-1950)

The linen industry's fortunes improved immensely during the American Civil War when the supply of raw cotton for its rival, the Belfast cotton industry, was greatly reduced. By 1868 ninety linen enterprises were in production in the Belfast area as well as textile finishing works and many of them were located along the banks of the Blackstaff. Other industries soon followed. A tobacco factory was opened in Linfield Road, reflective of the continuing links with the southern states of the United States despite the demise of the cotton industry in Belfast. (Jones, 1960) Fig 11.1

Belfast was a relatively compact town in the 1850s. Large-scale housing development for the increasing work force had yet to break out from the core residential areas of Millfield, Shankill and Sandy Row. There were two reasons for this. Firstly, mill workers were forced to live close to their places of employment because of their early starting times and long hours of work. Secondly, even the middle classes were restricted in the distance they could travel from their places of work in the town. It was not until the Turnpike Abolition Act 1837 that the middle classes felt free to commute daily into the town from residences beyond the tollgates. Up until then only the more affluent could live in scattered suburban villas and terrace groupings. (Cleary, 1983)

To cater for the needs of the influx of workers seeking employment in the mills many houses were needed, a demand that led to the building of street after street of houses in the lower Donegall Road, Grosvenor Road and Sandy Row area. Some of the houses were built by the factory owners near to the places of work at rents the workers could afford. The Malcolmsons of the Blackstaff Works, Broadway Weaving Company and Murphy & Stevenson of Sandy Row all became builders of basic quality homes. Additional houses were constructed by builders such as James McCurdy who encroached upon the Bog Meadows to build houses at Tavanagh Street. Other builders operated on a grander scale such as Hugh Scott who erected in 1894 over three hundred houses in Colchester, Dorchester, Barrington and Abington Streets on a site between the railway and Donegall Road. (Cleary, 1983)

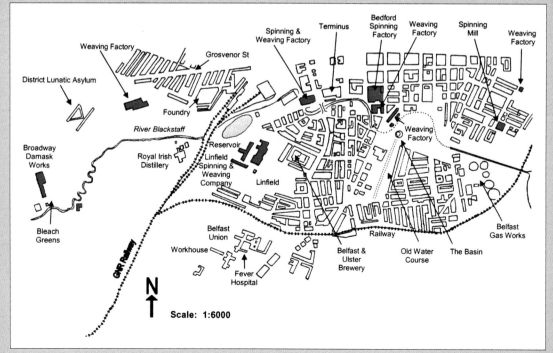

Fig 11.1 The distribution of linen and associated industries along the Blackstaff River in the latter half of the 19th century

In order to maximise the space available on the banks of the river, the channel was straightened at different places and the factory walls built so close to the water's edge that in effect the walls of the premises became the banks. This gave to the owners of the factories riparian rights that they exercised to get rid of unwanted liquids and other substances downstream adding to the dyes and chemicals emanating from the Milltown operation.

The growth of industry along the Blackstaff was an outward expansion of the old industrial cores around the Cromac Bridge near the Lagan and the Saltwater Bridge at Sandy Row. By the turn of the century it reached a point however when it could no longer extend westwards without major reclamation works on the wetlands of the Bog Meadows. The only enterprises that ventured to the edge of the Bog Meadows in later times were Kennedy Brothers who opened a dairy at Tate's Avenue on reclaimed ground and Clarence Engineering Company who built car repair works beside the river on a raised floor a short distance away from the dairy but more at risk from the flooding hazard.

The Clarence Engineering Works provided technical assistance to Juan Manuel Fangio when he competed in the Ulster Trophy race at Dundrod in 1951. Fangio's racing car experienced engine problems during practice runs at Dundrod and was taken to the workshop at the Bog Meadows for repair. Residents in the nearby streets who had to endure the early morning calls of the corncrake were awakened by the roar of the new engine as Fangio practiced on the open cinder-covered ground around the workshop. Unfortunately the repairs did not result in a victory lap as Fangio failed to make the podium!

In an age when few people expressed concern for the environment, the wetlands of the Bog Meadows were regarded by the Corporation as a convenient dumping ground for the city's refuse as well as providing building land. Several sites were chosen along the edge of the area, and were used continuously for this purpose until large areas were artificially raised above flood level. These areas became earmarked later for industrial expansion. Other organisations and companies contributed to the reshaping of the wetlands landscape. The Great Northern Railway Company had long since filled in several acres of wetland on which were placed the marshalling yards and engine sheds for the expanding railway system at Adelaide. The erosion of much of the Bog Meadows by different forms of development must have caused a degree of apprehension on the part of the few farming families that survived the radical changes that had taken place in the area since the beginning of the 19th century.

CHAPTER 12
Roads, Rail and Canal

The alignment of the Blackstaff presented problems to the earliest settlers who had chosen the narrow peninsula between it and the Farset as a site for a settlement. The lower course of the Farset was narrow and deep, easily bridged at different points to gain access to the other side and was navigable for smaller ships to tie up along the river banks in the tidal waters. The Blackstaff in contrast followed a twisting, meandering path from the southwest until it reached within a short distance from the Farset when it turned sharply at right angles to enter the Lagan 200 metres south of the mouth of the Farset. The tidal waters from Belfast Lough entered the lower reaches for a distance of 500 metres to a point where the land narrows between the Malone Ridge and the slightly higher ground of the town. This tidal limit marked later by the Ordnance Survey as *Highest Point to which Ordinary Tides Flow* was the lowest bridging point that could be crossed in safety. As a result it practically isolated the early settlement of Belfast from its southern approaches and restricted expansion in that direction. This bridge over the Blackstaff was of strategic importance in the early years of the 17th century causing Arthur Chichester to plan for its defence as well as the ford over the Lagan by building a large brick castle at Belfast upon *'the Rwynes of the decayed Castle (that was completed in 1610) ... the castle will defend the passage between the upper and lower Clandeboye and likewise the bridge over the River of Owenvarra between Malone and Belfast'*.

In 1625 Arthur Chichester died and was succeeded by his brother Edward, Viscount Chichester of Carrickfergus. He constructed a new bridge across the Blackstaff consisting of three arches and named it *'The Great Bridge of Belfast'* The structure received its first major lest when Colonel Venables, Commander of Oliver Cromwell's army marched north from Drogheda. He brought with him a baggage train complete with heavy guns, crossed over the river and seized the town. The bridge had to be repaired afterwards. With the building of the Long Bridge over the Lagan with its 21 arches in 1685 the word 'Great' was dropped and the bridge became known as 'Brickhill bridge'

after the nearby 'Brick Pitts'. (Moore, 1951).

Another army some 45 years later crossed over the bridge with the same intention of capturing the town. This time it was an Irish army of King James II who succeeded in taking the town for a short period. He then retreated across the bridge as the army of Schomberg advanced from north Down in hot pursuit. The strength of the arches was again put to the test as the heavy cannon were dragged across it by teams of horses. Its name appears to have been changed some years later when it became known as the *"Saltwater bridge"* in acknowledgement of the point where the tidal waters of the estuary went no farther. In 1717 the Grand Jury made an assessment for building buttresses "to support the Saltwater bridge and for other repairs above the bridge" (Young, 1896). The bridge lacked a footpath and used angular recesses or niches above the piers.

Apart from facilitating the movement of men, animals and cannon, the bridge was used to carry water pipes across to serve the needs of the town's population. The remains of these wooden pipes were discovered when a new bridge christened the *'Boyne Bridge'* was built across the river in 1935.

The bridge across the Blackstaff witnessed the comings and goings of herdsmen and traders bringing their cattle, sheep and goods for sale at markets outside the walls of the settlement at the mouth of the Farset. It witnessed the approach of Kings and Generals but surprisingly it was not the scene of any major battle despite its strategic location, but it did become the scene of sectarian rioting between mobs from the Catholic Pound Loney and Protestants from Sandy Row in 1864. In more recent times, the bridge retained something of its former strategic importance when protests were mounted at the foot of the bridge against outsiders, coming in to buy property in Sandy Row.

It is a concrete structure bereft of any architectural merit. It is purely the product of a functional design with no originality in its form. It straddles the railway and the river but from an historical perspective it hides all that has happened at this crossing of ages past. All that is left are memories written down in journals and maps that bear scant testimony to the momentous events at this crossing where the tidal waters reached.

Canal along the Blackstaff

The town of Belfast was hemmed in on the south by the low-lying marsh of the Blackstaff wetlands. It was linked by only one direct route to Lisburn and the Lough Neagh basin beyond. This routeway left the town along Barrack Street and Sandy Row crossing the Blackstaff over a narrow bridge build from the stones of the Long Bridge that had collapsed under the weight of the heavy cannon of Williamite forces that crossed over the Lagan prior to the battle of the Boyne. From Sandy Row horses and carts carried goods up a steep embankment to the Malone, to Lisburn and other places via a tortuous, winding road that followed closely the twists and turns of the Lagan river. This road made no attempt to go around the drumlins of Lambeg and Drumbridge, but instead went directly over them.

As a port, Belfast was experiencing increased volume of goods arriving at the quays for conveyance to places outside the town and it urgently needed better access routes to the Lough Neagh lowlands. It was partly for this reason that plans were drawn up to build a canal using the bed of the river and several locks to raise the level of the water in the canal to bring barges and lighters into Lisburn. This water highway was completed in 1763. The ultimate intention was to connect Belfast with Lough Neagh and all the possible commerce that that would generate. The river Lagan proved, however, to be unsuitable for this venture with severe flooding in winter and shortage of water in the summer being the main problems. So serious was the issue that Robert Whitworth, an English engineer was consulted by the Commissioners of Inland Navigation. He was not very encouraging about the existing canal and its dependence on the waters of the Lagan. Instead he proposed that a new canal be built all the way from Belfast to Lough Neagh but this time via a route that would take the navigation through the Blackstaff lowlands. His survey of 1768 suggested that the new alignment would utilise the abandoned estuarine mouth of the old river at Joy's paper mill and follow a new cut crossing the Blackstaff and head directly to Lisburn via Dunmurry. Fig 12.1 (P42)

The route this proposed navigation was to follow would have seen lighters laden with "coal, timber herrings, salt, tea, sugar, spirits, iron, bleaching stuffs etc. and large quantities of foreign timber on rafts" being pulled along slowly by horses towards Dunmurry crossing the Blackstaff a short distance up from Joy's paper mill and then paralleling the river until it crossed it again at Balmoral. On the return journey these canal boats would have carried building materials - sand, bricks and fireclay goods from Tyrone. Such a scheme would have altered dramatically the lands around the Blackstaff and opened them up to further exploitation. However, despite the gloomy report of Whitworth on the condition of the existing navigation along the Lagan, the Commissioners had neither the funds, nor the will to undertake such drastic measures and the whole idea was abandoned. It is conceivable that such an undertaking would have proved to be more profitable than the Lagan navigation down through the years. Furthermore such works may have avoided the fate that befell part of the Lagan navigation when the M1 was built. Some ten kilometres of the Lagan navigation was obliterated to allow the construction of the new motorway to proceed.

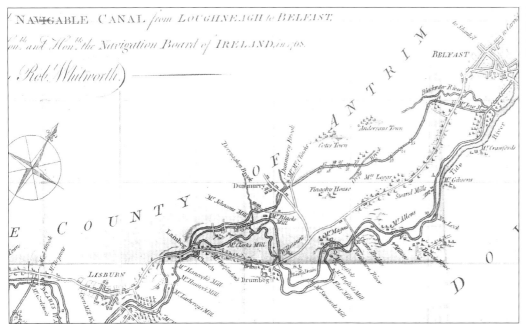

Fig 12.1 *Whitworth's Map of 1768 shows two possible alignments, one of which begins at Joy's Mill and makes its way towards Dunmurry parallelling the Blackstaff River.*

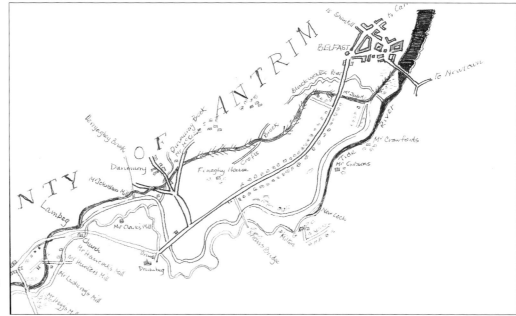

Fig 12.2 *Excerpt from Whitworth's Map 1768. It highlights the area shown on the original plan above. The planned canal through the Bog Meadows is drawn in solid blue along with the twelve locks required to make it operational from Belfast to Lambeg.*

Ulster Railway

Ironically, it was the Ulster Railway Company that took advantage of the route proposed by Whitworth. The Belfast to Lisburn section of track was opened in 1839. The line took two years to complete during inclement weather conditions which persisted during the summer months making the laying of the track along the edge of the Bog Meadows over the "sleech" very difficult especially since each engine weighed fifteen tons. Extensive infilling was required to provide a solid foundation for the marshalling yards at Adelaide and various outbuildings to service the needs of this new form of transportation. When the railway became operational, passengers had a panoramic view of the Bog Meadows and the South Antrim Hills in the distance. Here they would have noted the extensive bleach greens on the slopes of the Black Mountain and Hannahstown Hill. (Benn, 1823)

On the other side of the line, looking towards to Malone Ridge, they would have noted several textile factories close to Sandy Row and the changes taking place along the new road leading to Lisburn 'NEW ROAD'. This road was laid down 10 years previous to the opening of the railway and reflected thee need for a shorter and easier route to Lisburn avoiding the problems mentioned earlier. It veered of from the Malone Road at the tollgate near Sandy Row and followed the 15 metre contour avoiding the wetlands of the Bog Meadows until it reached the linen village of Dunmurry. It then proceeded directly to Lisburn shortening the distance from Belfast to Lisburn by a distance of five kilometres compared to the old route via the Malone Road.

As a result of the new road and railway line the long elongated farms which had characterised the Malone ridge were broken up with the lower slopes becoming wedges of land lying in between the Lisburn Road, the Ulster Railway and the Bog Meadows. Much of this land at the lower side of the Lisburn Road became the focus of speculative housing in the latter part of the 19th century. The proximity of the industrial area around Sandy Row ensured the need for more artisan dwellings, the result of which was the building of many streets of terraced houses between the road and the railway up as far as Balmoral. These streets of terraced housing extended the industrial sector of Sandy Row and were populated by people similar in religion and occupations.

If the Malone Road acted as a physical watershed between the valley of the Blackstaff and the River Lagan the Lisburn Road acted as a social watershed or 'social precipice' as described by Jones (1954) between the opulence of the villas and the houses of the gentry in the Malone side and the crowded streets of artisans houses on the other side of the road. A comparison between the occupations of some of the people in the streets opposite each other emphasises the difference. In Adelaide Avenue in 1914, according to the Belfast Street Directory for that year, there lived a caulker, joiner, two engine drivers, two boilermakers, a baker and a gardener. In Adelaide Park there lived a company director, a doctor, two solicitors, an estate agent, a dentist and a Justice of the Peace. In effect. the character of the Malone ridge was predetermined by its early history of settlement, and socially the Lisburn Road became the accepted limit of this sector. The land between the Lisburn road and the Bog Meadows was less desirable because of its low lying nature. Much of it was eventually given over to public institutions such as the Fever Hospital and the Workhouse, the Deaf and Dumb Institute and the Malone Industrial School. Such institutions were matched on the other side of the Bog Meadows along the Falls Road with the Royal Hospital, Lunatic Asylum and the Industrial School at Milltown.

The general directions of roads, railway and canal from Belfast southwards reflected a parallel alignment with the Blackstaff River and floodplain. This pattern continued into the 20th century when the M1 motorway and Boucher Road followed the same north-south alignment with Stockman's Lane and Donegall Road acting as cross-valley routes as had been the case in the past.

CHAPTER 13
Traditions and Troubles

As the town expanded and encroached upon the wetlands of the Blackstaff around its estuarine mouth, the population increased in like proportion. The youth of the day took advantage of the new cut to swim and bathe in the river and to sail in the abandoned portion that functioned as a dam for Joy's paper mill. Others ventured farther back along the river to collect edible plants, look for bird's nests and pick wild flowers that grew in abundance. In late January groups of young people and old would venture out into the Bog Meadows to cut rushes for St Brigid's Day, February 1st. These rushes would be shaped into crosses to honour the second in order of importance of the saints, of Ireland - "Mary of the Irish". These crosses would be fashioned into complicated and intricate forms often in school to decorate altars and to hang in a prominent place at home. It was in these open fields that local May customs took place each year in which two traditions were kept. On May Eve after the sun had gone down, young people would congregate in and around the fields where they would collect flowers and generally enjoy themselves. The young women would attempt to find out something about their future husband by either inspecting a trail laid down by a snail or by picking a bunch of yarrow that would induce dreams in which her future husband would be revealed. Yarrow was believed to have the capacity to improve the looks of a young woman and protect her from harm. On May Day young people collected flowers made wreaths and decorated bushes and poles.

The Bog Meadows lay in between the Catholic Pound and Protestant Sandy Row. It became the meeting ground for both Catholic and Protestant youths and at the turn of the19th century there were no reports of any animosity between them as they engaged in May activities. At this time sectarian violence was absent in Belfast and the town enjoyed a reputation for religious tolerance. It must be pointed out, however, that Catholics accounted for only 10% of the population. As the industrial and commercial base of the town increased and the rural economy declined more and more people migrated from the countryside a movement that increased steadily the proportion of Catholics in the population. These new migrants brought with them their memories and experiences of faction fighting in rural Ulster and the sectarian strife that had gripped parts of the province. There was consequently a great deal of unease amongst the Protestant population at the prospect of the town becoming increasingly Catholic. Added to this fear of numbers was the increasingly truculent campaign of Daniel O'Connell for Catholic Emancipation. The first sign of troubles that were to plague the town in the first half of the 19th century began in 1813 with a riot between Catholics and Protestants. Other riots occurred throughout the 1830s.

The May festivities remained largely unaffected by the periodic outbursts of sectarian violence. In a report in the Belfast News Letter of 1861 the occasion was celebrated by a large cross-section of the people.

"Yesterday, being May Eve, in accordance with the very ancient custom in Ireland, large numbers of the younger portion of the community assembled in the fields in the outskirts of the town to enjoy an evening's amusement, and for the purpose of gathering May flowers. As usual, on occasions where numbers of both sexes are met, there was no lack of fun and all tried to enjoy themselves and succeeded, and no accidents occurred to mar the sport." (Kinealy, 1981)

By 1864, however, things began to change. The sectarian riots of that year impacted upon the festivities of the following May and the Bog Meadows witnessed clashes between rival groups from the Pound and Sandy Row. On May Eve 1865 the age-old custom of collecting flowers to decorate bushes and trees was interrupted by verbal abuse that was soon followed by stone throwing between youths from different sides. With the arrival of the police both sides dispersed but they reformed for an even bigger confrontation at Sandy Row later in the day. A large force of police numbering twenty was sent in to disperse them but was met with a fusillade of stones that seriously injured a number of them. Reinforcements were sent in to clear the area. The following day in court several rioters were brought before the magistrate and

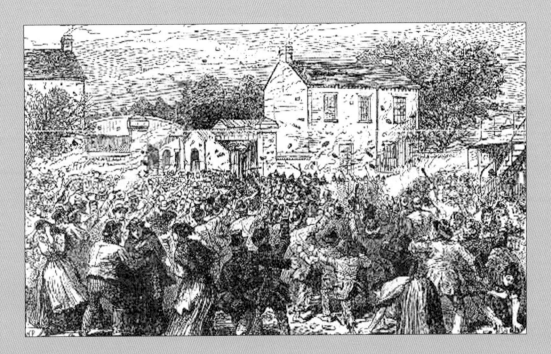

Fig. 13.1 *Mob wrecking the tramway company's depot at Milltown (Illustrated London News, 21 August 1886) The presence of so many Unionist supporters at Milltown is not surprising given the distribution of the Protestant population of Belfast in the 1880s. (Radford, 1999).*

sentenced to two months hard labour. Others were fined for using abusive language and party expressions such as 'to hell with the Pope' and ' to hell with King William'. Even the police were subject to name calling such as 'Papish Peelers'! (Kinealy, 1990)

The following year, the police planned to curb any repeat of the previous year's confrontation by sending a large contingent to the Bog Meadows before the crowds arrived. In the early evening after the mills closed, large numbers of young people assembled at the Bog Meadows to gather May flowers. Around seven in the evening hundreds gathered in the fields enjoying themselves during which 'the greatest order and good humour prevailed until about dusk'. It was too good to last. Shortly after 8 o'clock,

the beating of Orange drums from the direction of the Lisburn Road attracted a rival group of Catholics youths to advance towards the river. Both sides engaged in booing and jeering each other followed by stone throwing. The police managed to intervene successfully and both sides went their separate ways, the Catholics by way of the Lunatic Asylum and the Protestants by way of the south bank of the Blackstaff as far as the Pound Mill. (Kinealy, 1990)

In 1867 things were quiet on May Eve, although this was more due to the bad weather as it had to do with the police presence in the Bog Meadows. On May Day young people again gathered wild flowers under the watchful eye of a large number of police. No incidents were reported. There was only an occasional skirmish between Protestant and Catholic youths during the following decade. In 1880 it was reported that there was some unrest among the assembled crowd as they gathered to collect flowers on May Eve. *'Yesterday evening, being May Eve, large numbers of persons repaired to the neighbourhood of the Bog Meadows for the purpose of gathering flowers. Great animation was displayed on all sides'*

By the 1880s the May traditions could no longer be enjoyed without the fear of sectarian riots between the rival groups. The religious divide was further deepened as the Home Rule campaign gathered momentum culminating in the violence after the election results of 1886. By this time the practice of *amaying* diminished in importance due to the risks involved in entering the Bog Meadows to gather May flowers and enjoy the fullness of Spring. Moreover, the practice of decorating bushes and trees with flowers and the making of wreaths for the house was linked to a more devotional practice by Catholics to honour the Virgin Mary. The month of May was dedicated to her by the Catholic Hierarchy and statues of the Virgin Mary were adorned with May flowers. The increasing manifestation of the 'devotional revolution' of the different Christian churches in the late decades of the 19th century meant that traditional customs and beliefs were increasingly absorbed into more exclusive forms of religious practice. The harvest festival of Lunasa was incorporated into the Catholic Feast of the Assumption celebrated on August 16th. Each year this date was marked by processions in the Falls area in which the statue of the Virgin Mary was carried aloft. In the evening, it was followed by the lighting of bonfires that were more of a riposte to the bonfires of the Twelfth of July than in veneration of the Virgin Mary. The effects of this new religious climate and political unrest was the erosion of traditional practices associated with the pagan feasts of Bealtaine and Lunasa. The common heritage of both Catholic and Protestant communities was being disregarded and the gulf between them widened by the turn of the century. This gulf continued throughout the twentieth century frustrating the desire of the youth of the 'Village' area to access the Black Mountain. Robert Harbinson was one of those who wished to explore the Black Mountain for the gold of Neeshy Haughan. It was inaccessible because he had to cross the territory of the Bog Meadows 'held by the Mickeys' (Harbinson, 1960).

CHAPTER 14

Winston Churchill's Visit to Celtic Park, 8th February, 1912.

Celtic Park or 'Paradise' with its covered accommodation provided an excellent facility for the soccer club and its mainly Catholic supporters from Belfast and elsewhere in the north of Ireland. Despite the political turmoil of the late 19th and early 20th centuries, there were no major incidents reported between rival supporters during or after games. Electric tramlines had been extended by 1912 along the Falls, Grosvenor and Donegall Roads to bring supporters from other parts of the town. Outside Celtic Park the tramcars lined up to convey supporters back into town and on to other outlying areas that helped reduce the risk of crowd trouble.

In February, 1912 Celtic Park was in the spotlight, not from some sporting event, but for acceding to the request from the Ulster Liberal Association to hold a demonstration in support of Home Rule during which it was to hear an address from the First Lord of the Admiralty, Winston Churchill and prominent Nationalist politicians such as Joe Devlin and John Redmond. It had been earlier planned to hold the demonstration in the Ulster Hall but such was the opposition from the Ulster Unionists that approaches were made to the club in the days leading up to that week to avoid confrontation. The Unionist supporters threatened to hold counter-demonstrations outside the hall to thwart any attempt by the Liberals to conduct such a meeting. In an interview with Captain Craig M.P., at Mount Stewart in January, the intentions of the Ulster Unionist Council were made clear if not the detail of their plans:

"I cannot reveal what steps are being taken, but I am one of those who are determined to see that the meeting will not take place under any circumstances, and that every possible ingenuity shall be displayed in preventing a rebel crew dishonouring that historic Ulster Hall".

The Ulster Liberal Association attempted to obtain permission to hold the meeting in an alternative building in the town centre but was unsuccessful. It was refused the use of Corporation halls, of the Opera House, Theatre Royal,

Willowfield Huts

the Hippodrome and other covered places. It then approached the custodians of Celtic Park to hold the meeting in the open air. When it succeeded in obtaining use of the ground it then withdrew its application for the Ulster Hall and announced its intention to go ahead with a demonstration at Celtic Park. Colonel R.W.Wallace, Grand Master of Belfast Orangemen then issued a statement or manifesto on Tuesday 6th asking its Brethren to abstain from interfering with the demonstration.

On the same day 3500 troops from the Curragh Command arrived from Dublin in six special trains adding to the local garrison of 2500 raising the military force in Belfast to 6000 men. Some of them, notably the Cyclist Corps attached to the East Kent Regiment (Buffs), seemed to have been assigned duties around Celtic Park that entailed all-night vigils around the ground.

"The small bundle of firewood carried by each of the men of the cyclist corps was grimly suggestive of street bivouacking."

They must have endured a miserable time guarding approaches

Fig. 14.1 *Soldiers in reserve on the Blackstaff Lane now called St. James's Park: The continuous rain made the experience very unpleasant for the military. Source: Daily Sketch Photographs.*

Figure 14.2 *The telephone box just outside Winston's tent to enable the speech to be reported Source: Daily Sketch Photographs.*

to the ground as the weather was atrocious judging from reports at the time. The photograph above shows soldiers of the East Kent Regiment stationed along Blackstaff Lane (St. James's Park) in the rain. Some of the officers and men may have been stationed in the Willowfield Huts nearby on the Falls Road which were erected to house the cavalry during the 1886 riots in Belfast (Baker, J., Kerr, R. 1994).

To provide accommodation for the numbers expected to attend the demonstration, a large marquee was erected in front of the grandstand in which the main speakers and guests would be seated and speeches made. Those outside the marquee would hear the different speakers by means of a sounding board erected in the roof of the tent above their heads. In an age when telephone technology was in its infancy, a special telephone system was installed as shown in the photograph to send reports to Manchester and other English towns.

The inside of the marquee and grandstand was draped with Union Jacks, a sight which would have been unthinkable in later times! The speakers, apart from Winston Churchill, included the Chairperson, Lord Pirrie, John Redmond and Joe Devlin. Over 8000 thousand people attended the demonstration far above the number of tickets issued for the meeting in the Ulster Hall. Although nationalist politicians were invited to speak, the Ulster Liberal association were at pains to emphasise that this was not a Nationalist demonstration. Indeed, on the previous Sunday in all Catholic churches in Belfast the congregations were exhorted not to go to Celtic park and to avoid the area all together. Despite this advice, hundreds of Nationalists queued up to pay one shilling to enter the unreserved side of the ground. Whatever the make-up of the crowd, they listened intently to the speeches and what was said and what was promised. Some were not content just to listen but interrupted Winston Churchill on several occasions with questions about women's suffrage. One member of the suffragettes, Mrs Convery was ejected from the hall. Throughout the day the rain continued to beat down on the tent and raised fears that at some stage it would collapse on the dignitaries underneath. Over and over again rain had to be removed from the roof surface by pushing upwards with brushes from the inside. Eventually all the speeches were delivered and the distinguished guests and the crowds outside stood to attention as the demonstration ended late in the afternoon in loyal song.

"The singing of the' National Anthem' brought an historic meeting to a glorious close" As the crowd dispersed by late afternoon under the protection of a large body of police and soldiers, no trams were available outside the ground that would have eased the cold and wet of those who had stood outside in the rain all afternoon and who had to journey into town.

The First Lord of the Admiralty travelled through Belfast with a military escort to the Midland Railway Station where he boarded a train for Larne and on to Scotland. His journey was compared to that of Daniel O' Connell 71 years previously in an article in the Belfast Evening Telegraph of 28th March, 1912.

"The recent visit of Mr. Winston Churchill to Belfast and his ignominious flight from 'Paradise' by way of the back streets to the special train for Larne

Harbour, and thence to Scotland, has a parallel to some extent with the visit of Mr Daniel O'Connell in January, 1841 when he also hurriedly fled from Belfast to Donaghadee and Portpatrick, to fulfil an engagement (as was alleged) to speak at a meeting of the Reform Club at Leeds, but, as a fact, he only arrived there some twenty four hours after the meeting took place.

So ended weeks of tension in Belfast when the Home Rule campaign was at its height. 'Paradise' returned to its normal use but from then on it was to be regarded in the Protestant and Unionist community as the home not only of a soccer club but as a symbol of Nationalist agitation. The club went out of its way to ensure that its players were selected on their skills as soccer players and not on their religion but despite those efforts over the coming decades, the 'green and whites' and their supporters were greeted with hostility in many loyalist areas until Belfast Celtic withdrew from the Irish League in 1948.

CHAPTER 15
Housing and Social Scene

Housing seemed to keep a jump ahead of industrial development partly due to the extension of the tramway system that had begun with the introduction of horse-trams in the 1880s to be replaced with electric trams in 1904. House building continued in what is now called 'the village' west of the railway line at the bottom of Tate's Avenue. With the advent of the First World War, however, house building almost ceased creating major problems for those people who came into Belfast seeking work in the munition factories and other employment. After the war, Belfast Corporation was forced to consider municipal housing because developers were unwilling to build houses for people who could afford only minimum rents. One of the building projects consisted of two hundred houses in the fields to the south of the Donegall Road in the 1920s. The streets were all called after St. James but never carried the apostrophe so that they became titled St James Road, Parade, Drive, Place, Gardens, and Crescent. (In this account the apostrophe s is added to conform with present nomenclature.) The rows of houses in Rodney Parade and Rodney Drive and St Katherine's Road were built later. Each street housed over forty families and the occupations of the tenants were as varied as the places in the north of Ireland from which they hailed from. There were shoemakers and shop assistants, barmen and bin collectors, tram drivers and train drivers, and painters and policemen. Some worked locally in different enterprises such as bakeries, mills and foundries. Many worked elsewhere in the numerous firms 'making up' textiles such as Albion Clothing and Atkinson's Tie factory. Others worked in the Globe and Monarch laundries. Some remained unemployed and lived on state benefits that were very meagre.

Because of the wide range of occupations, there was a gradation of socio-economic rank from one street to the next. In the upper streets of St James's Parade and Drive there were more self-employed and professional people. The streets of Rodney Parade and Rodney Crescent had more manual workers. This gradation was matched on the Lisburn Road side of the Bog Meadows

only the distinction was more evident. In ways the contour lines conformed to what was referred to in chapter 13 as 'a social precipice' namely as one proceeded down slope, one encountered more lower income groups.

The bond between the people living in the St James's Road area and Tate's Avenue in terms of their occupations was offset by their differences in religious affiliation. The people of the upper Donegall Road were mainly Catholic and the residents of the lower Donegall Road were mainly Protestant. Their religious loyalties were often evident in the support they gave to Belfast Celtic and Linfield soccer clubs on Saturday afternoons. The matches acted as a release mechanism for the working classes in both communities as well as from farther afield. As fortune would have it, the grounds were within 'a stone's throw' of each other but the supporters tended to congregate at the end nearest to their home areas on either side of the Blackstaff and usually dispersed peacefully when the matches were over. Belfast Celtic had moved from their first ground at Brighton Street to a ten-acre' green field' site on the Donegall Road in 1896 long before housing development had taken place in the area. It was made available to other sports as well as soccer. In the summer there were open-air boxing tournaments. At other times of the year there was pony-trotting, whippet racing and athletics.

Linfield moved from the Meadow at Linfield Mill off Sandy Row to several other grounds before finally settling at Windsor Park in 1905. In the years of the new century there was constant political turmoil over the Home Rule campaign especially in Belfast. This tension was evident at sporting events such as was seen at Solitude, the home ground of Cliftonville when rival supporters clashed in 1908. There was also an outbreak of crowd trouble at Celtic Park a few years later during a match with Bohemians. In 1912, however, Belfast Celtic made national headlines not for its exploits on the field of play but because the directors agreed to a request from the Ulster Liberal Association to hold a meeting in the grounds as outlined in the previous chapter.

At a lower level of competition there were numerous local clubs who did not possess their own grounds but were content to play on any open area that was suitable. The Bog Meadows provided enough space for several pitches, one at the end of Rodney Parade and the other at the rear of Windsor Park. Even other smaller patches of waste ground could be used for scratch teams to engage in playing a game of soccer. Some of these games were played as part of a formal league organised by local clubs who could rely on a large support for each of their fixtures. In the Falls League, there were teams who often used local street names to distinguish them from the rest. Alton United, Bath Rangers and St.Peter's Swifts were some of the sides that competed for many years in this league.

Those who followed Gaelic Games had to travel a little farther to Shaun's Park on the Whiterock Road or the playing fields in the Falls Park. Soccer was more popular among the working class of the Falls as the Gaelic revival had yet to gain popular support. Under the influence of the Christian Brothers and the De La Salle Brothers, schools began to field both Gaelic football and hurling teams. A Schools League saw teams from all over the city competing. The Farney Cup was a knock-out competition which saw great rivalry between schools such as St Finian's and St Galls. One of the strongest sides was fielded by the De La Salle Brothers who were in charge of St.Patrick's Industrial School at Milltown. The 'home boys' as they were affectionately known were 'semi-professional' in the sense that they were out training almost every day in a field which had been laid out over filled material and then grassed over to make an excellent playing surface. Visiting sides were intimidated by the skills and strength of the commitment which they encountered from the 'home boys', many of whom could have become county stars if they had continued to play Gaelic games after they left the sanctuary of the 'home'. The excellent guidance that the Brothers gave the players was matched by the professional manner in which they exercised control over the school to which the boys were sent by the courts. St. Patrick's Industrial School, which was its official title, was based in Milltown House,

the former residence of a Belfast merchant. It had use of the old beetling mill that was converted to a hostel for those sent by the courts. A gate lodge greeted visitors at the Falls Road entrance, but access could be gained by a flight of steps that carried the visitor over the Ballymurphy River to the yard outside the converted beetling mill. In it the boys were trained in assorted skills including tailoring and shoe-repair, which it was hoped would help them in later life.

The residents of the St James's area, who wished for more leisurely activities, had a choice. The children could play a range of street games while both children and adults could pay into several cinemas that had opened nearby such as the Broadway, the Windsor or the Majestic on the Lisburn Road. In an age when wages were low and many people were out of work the temptation to gamble was very strong be it on cock-fights or the odd dog-fight (Fleming, 1998). A number of bookmakers had premises in the vicinity and Celtic Park organised dog racing two nights a week with the same bookmakers taking bets at their individual stalls. Many gamblers were not satisfied with such provision and gathered at different places to play 'pitch and toss', a form of gambling which was illegal. Large crowds gathered at the weekend to try their luck on the two coins that were tossed into the air. One such 'school' of 'punters' and onlookers assembled at the rear of Clarence Engineering Works to try their fortune on the even money bet that the same side of two different coins would turn up when they hit the ground after being tossed into the air. This form of gambling was based on very simple rules and could be played with small numbers or a large group of 'punters'. It was 'minded' by local tough men such as Barney Ross and Silver McKee (Fleming, 1998). The game required some one who was willing to 'cover' the bets with his money. In doing so, he then took charge of the toss. In the toss, two coins, usually half pennies, were tossed into the air, sometimes from a flat piece of wood. Occasionally, a piece of bone would serve as the base. The person who tossed the coins, hoped that two 'heads'

Fig 15.1 *'Pitch' and 'Toss' school in action, behind Clarence's Engineering Premises in the Bog Meadows.*

would be turned up when the coins hit the ground. He would then lift all the money that was placed on the ground in a circle next to the person who laid the bet. The punters hoped instead for two 'harps' that was the name of the opposite side of the coins. A 'head' and a 'harp' would mean that the coins were tossed another time. If one of the punters thought that the coins were not tossed properly, he could shout out 'call them'. This would cancel the toss and the coins would have to be tossed again. Large sums of money were won and lost at this form of gambling. If the person who tossed the coins could succeed in turning over two 'heads' consistently three or four times, the end result would be a complete clean-up of the punters' money. Often both sides would be on the losing end if the RUC suddenly descended on the 'pitch' and lift what was still on the ground! Fig 15.1

For those who could not afford the price for the cinema or other indoor entertainment, winter was a problem. The only alternative on a rainy winter's night, other than sitting in, was to gain shelter somewhere and spend the night standing talking and sharing a cigarette with friends. Often the shelter was the gable end of a row of houses where the roof extended beyond the houses and one could stand under the eaves to gain some protection. If the rain ceased or eased off, then a decision would be made to 'go for a walk' which would usually entailed setting out at a brisk pace up to the Falls Road and out towards Suffolk to return via the Glen Road. On a rare occasion, they might have been allowed into someone's house to share in a cup of hot Oxo or Bovril on their return.

Winters were long and hard to endure in an age when few had cars and central heating was a luxury that did not exist in council housing. These hardships were made worse by the frequent winter fogs that occurred. At night, the colder denser air on the upper slopes of the Black Mountain descended into the low ground of the Bog Meadows displacing aloft the warmer air from the hundreds of chimneys. This produced a downslope wind that in turn condensed the moisture in the air forming fog. In the streets off the Donegall Road this temperature inversion trapped the particulates and pollutants from the chimney smoke converting the cold air at lower levels into smog. For many of the residents such conditions aggravated chest and heart complaints especially among those who smoked cigarettes and pipe tobacco. Often the cold was intense enough to freeze the open waters of the Bog Meadows allowing the more adventurous to walk or skate on the ice. The steep slope of St James Road provided a frozen surface for makeshift toboggans to slide at speed down to the bottom at St James Place much to the discomfort of the residents crossing the road!

Traveller families often camped in the Bog Meadows and stayed for long periods in the open areas at the bottom of St James's Road and St Katherines's Road. They arrived in horse-drawn caravans reminiscent of those of the Wild West. The main difference between them was the extent to which they decorated the outside of their wooden frames with a variety of colours and designs such that each travelling family was distinguished from the others. They were all part of an extended family group identified by their surname such as McDonagh. As a social group, the 'tinkers' as they were called then, tended to be regarded as a nuisance by the local residents accusing them of pilfering and stealing anything they could get their hands on. They also went around the streets calling at doors asking for money, food or clothes. Once settled on a particular halting site, they released the horses called piebalds to graze on the surrounding

meadows. In most cases, makeshift tents were erected nearby and these were used as sleeping quarters for young and old alike. Open fires provided the heat needed for cooking and comfort during the night. The young people from the nearby streets had strange fascination for their lifestyle as the traveller children did not appear to attend school for one thing. They also displayed a contempt for the mores of the time and showed a certain cockiness and independence in their behaviour. They were also regarded as being able to tell fortunes and predict the future of those willing to extend their hands for their palms to be read. On one occasion, word went around that in one of the caravans there was a talking crow. That was sufficient information to entice some of the children to venture over to the campsite in the hope of seeing and hearing the crow. One of the children was bold enough to ask if there was a talking crow and to their surprise a cage was brought out for them to see the big black crow inside. One of the older women engaged the crow in conversation by calling out certain commands. The crow replied much like a parrot. In addition, the woman had the ability to cast her voice to deceive the children into believing it had greater fluency than a parrot! Needless to say everyone was impressed and went home in the certainty that the crow could talk.

15.2 Children assembled around the 'talking crow'.

Children abandoning the derelict caravan as it speeds down St. James's Road

When the head of a family unit died it was customary for the travellers to set fire to his caravan and burn all his personal possessions. On one occasion this occurred in the Bog Meadows and when the fire burned out all the travellers left after pushing the remains of the shell of the caravan into the edge of the marsh. The following day several of the local youths decided to pull the chassis out of the water. For this they needed strong ropes and a larger number of people to succeed in retrieving what remained of the caravan. One of the youths that had joined in the task collected ropes as a sort of pastime from those cast aside by many of the drivers of the horse drawn carts that still hauled goods throughout the city. These ropes were attached to the rear axle of the caravan and with everyone pulling from the back the caravan was brought to dry land. The iron-shod wheels were still sound and could turn as effectively as before. With some more effort the caravan was dragged out on to the road and inspected. The axles at the front and rear were untouched by the fire and the two shafts were also unaffected. The decision was made to harness several of the young boys to the shafts with others at the back of the caravan to help push it up the hill at the top of St James's Road. The caravan started to move and with its momentum increasing as it was pushed and pulled it eventually was hauled up to the top of the hill and turned around with great difficulty to face the downward slope. It was necessary for some boys to hold on to the ropes to prevent it from taking off on its own. When all were ready the remainder of the youths climbed on board and set off down the hill. The caravan slowly gained speed and everyone yelled in delight as it rolled down the hill but after a few moments panic set in as the caravan gained speed despite the efforts of those holding on from behind to stop it from accelerating. Half way down the hill those who were watching from the pavement including several women and children ran for cover as the half burnt caravan flew past. Fortunately it came to rest at the bottom of the road minus a few of its passengers who either jumped in panic or were thrown off sustaining cuts and bruises for their efforts.

Some of the men of the area succeeded in removing the caravan to a safer place at the waste ground at Clarence's Engineering Works where it remained for some days before it was removed by someone who may have used it for carrying goods elsewhere in the town.

CHAPTER 16
Triumph and Tragedy

With the building of new housing estates after the First World War along the top end of the Donegall Road and the bottom of Tate's Avenue, a new generation grew up with the Bog Meadows a short distance from them. It became a playground for the children of the area and an attractive environment for the people of the area who had earlier resided in congested districts of the town. Access was by means of the raised ditches along the drainage channels or directly down the country lanes that led off from the Falls Road. Despite its reduced size from what it was in the past, in the minds of the children it seemed to stretch far into the distance towards Stockman's Lane. Between the Donegall Road and Stockman's Lane lay hundreds of acres of fields, and farmyards separated by numerous water channels and hedgerows. Into this rural wonderland wandered children and youths of all ages collecting flowers or plants or birds' eggs as well as those who enjoyed playing in the fields or wandering about with no particular purpose. In springtime the Bog Meadows became alive with plants and flowers of every description and the scent from the grasses and wild flowers drifted across the nearby streets to remind the residents of the countryside next door. Crossing over the ditches that separated the fields in springtime was an exhilarating experience. The ground was covered with a carpet of flowering plants, rushes, sedges and tall grasses. Many of the flowers grew along the edge of the wetlands whilst others preferred the open meadowlands. As Goode remarked *'if Belfast children are city born, it is their good luck not to be street-bred. They have the key of the fields, and the least adventurous of them roam far and wide.'* (Good, 1919).

The more adventurous would seek out other challenges that the Bog Meadows could offer, challenges that natural obstacles would present to them. One such challenge centred on the *'corner jump'*, a place where two streams joined together and where the water at that point was deep. The distance across this confluence was nearly two metres, but the approach to the jump from the inner bank was steep and the opposite bank was a little higher. If the jumper failed to leap across, he would be guaranteed a wet and muddy bath. Few ever succeeded, and those who did were well known in the local annals. Most who were brave enough to test their jumping abilities usually faced the prospect of explaining their wet state at home. Fig 16.1

Climbing was a more straightforward pursuit especially if they were fruit trees to be climbed. Those residents who had apple or pear orchards or rows of raspberries and gooseberries usually protected their gardens with a stout fence but often it did not deter some of the more determined teenagers from getting across and enjoying the fruits of summer. Sometimes they were caught in the act and on a rare occasion faced a summons when the angry resident reported the offence to the police at Andersonstown.

Such was the risk in climbing fruit trees, or trying to jump over a river channel, but the risk of not succeeding did not merit a severe penalty other than a fine in court which rarely happened. Risk assessment was rarely taken into account when a challenge came the way of a young person and on more than one occasion such an assessment might well have avoided the heartbreak that some families had to endure as the result of accidents which occurred in the area. One incident illustrates how a moment's indecision or a step too far could result in death or serious injury.

Bobby McCrudden from St. James's Road and his friends strolled down to the Blackstaff to watch as engineers from the Northern Ireland Electricity Board set about raising electricity cables into position between the two tall metal pylons located between Rodney Parade and the river. Each pylon carried the weight of eight cables that were intended to carry power to other parts. The cables were attached to each pylon and were swinging to and fro near ground level as the engineers went off to the rear of Celtic Park to switch on the engine that would raise the cables to the required height. When they left the scene Bobby McCrudden and his friends jumped up and grabbed one of the cables and began to swing on it. Within a few minutes the cable started to rise and everyone let go except Bobby. He held on until the cable had reached its highest point. One of his companions raced across to warn the engineers of his plight but before they had time to react, Bobby could no longer hold on and fell to the ground. The impact killed him.

CHAPTER 17
Agriculture in the Bog Meadows

The Bog Meadows was not the sole preserve of the local residents and their children. The fields provided lush grass for beef and dairy cattle. Cattle were shipped in from distant farms and given a short period to rest and gain weight before being sent to the abattoir. The McGovern brothers of Erindale owned land stretching from the Falls Road to the Blackstaff and had 60 to 70 head of cattle in the fields. They would buy and sell 100 to 150 head of cattle each week with the farmyard acting as sort of auction. As well as cattle, the brothers reared pigs and in the farm buildings there were stalls for over 600 animals.

Collin's farm, one of the largest in the district, had a large dairy herd.

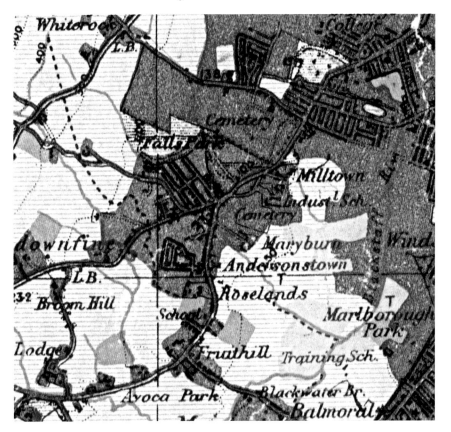

Fig. 17.1 *Land-use map of Bog Meadows and surrounding area (based on Land Utilisation Map of Northern Ireland. HMSO). Scale 1:15000. Note (a) the small area of orchards and gardens in Milltown; (b) the cultivated area (possibly oats) in Collins farm between Fruithill and Roselands. Note as well the area under cultivation at the Training School; (c) the extent of pasture and meadow land in the Bog Meadows; (d) the large area of marsh and lowland bog.*

ORCHARDS, GARDENS, ETC.
Orchards, gardens, allotments, nurseries, farmsteads with gardens, housing estates.........................

LAND AGRICULTURALLY UNPRODUCTIVE
Areas agriculturally unproductive, including buildings, yards, cemeteries, lowland bog, etc.....................

WOODLANDS
Woodland, coniferous and deciduous.............................

ARABLE LAND
Land under crops, small fruit and market garden products..............................

GRASSLANDS
Land under grass including rotation grass, permanent pasture and meadowland ....

HEATH AND MOORLAND
Rough grassland, rough mountain pasture, upland bog and sea-saltings..............................

The farmstead was situated just south of Milltown cemetery and was called Maryburn. It stretched down to the riverbank of the Blackstaff. The herd was a mixture of Jersey and Friesian breeds and produced high- grade milk.

Much of the area was categorised as permanent pasture or meadowland. Small patches were devoted to crops and market garden produce. Collin's Farm has a large field set aside for cereals for his herd of cattle and pigs. Other users included the Malone Industrial School which had set aside two fields for the young men to grow vegetables, flowers and tomatoes for use in the school kitchen. North of this establishment the land was under water until the railway embankment was   reached which ran parallel to the line of the Blackstaff. On this reclaimed land, which the corporation had used as a landfill site, the Adelaide Marshalling yards and engineering sheds were sited. On the edges of the tracks, many of the rail workers had plots on which to grow vegetables, flowers and in the greenhouses tomatoes for their own consumption or for sale to their fellow workers.

On the Falls Road side of the Bog Meadows there were several small patches of land given over to allotments or 'plots' which were an important resource providing fresh vegetables, flowers and tomatoes for the local community and a rewarding occupation for young and old alike. For the older men of the district it provided an outdoor activity and a focal point where they could meet each other and share their problems and experiences about growing particular plants and anything else besides. Between the Broadway Damask factory and the river there were rows of plots laid out in a line along the riverbank. A much larger allotment stretched down from Clondara Street to the Bog Meadows and was divided up into different plots leased out to local residents. It was crisscrossed with narrow paths to take people to

different locations and different glasshouses within which tomatoes and early vegetables were grown. Access to the plots was limited to one entrance from St James's Road and the allotment was protected by the marshland surrounding it. Figure 17.1.

CHAPTER 18
The War Years

The advent of the Second World War caused the sectarian tensions to ease along the interface between the Catholic and Protestant communities on both sides of the Blackstaff River. For the first time, Catholic and Protestant working class families found themselves up against a common threat when war broke out. Many men and women from both sides responded to the need for recruits to the British armed forces. Many found work in Mackies engineering works making munitions, or in other war work. The older generation joined auxiliary organisations such as the ARP (Air Raid Precautions) to act as wardens in the event of air raids. They were given training in First Aid and expected to take control over civilian movements in the event of an attack. They knew the location of the various air raid shelters and the location of First Aid Posts. They had the task of directing civilians to these places and to ensure that this was done in an orderly way. The local unit of the ARP were housed in the Directors' Rooms in Celtic Park.

In order to minimise the risk of the Luftwaffe detecting the location of targets, a blackout was enforced and the ARP sought to maintain this in the city streets. Each house we given gas masks for the people inside and sandbags to put out fires from incendiaries. Water tanks were built: one at the end of St James's Crescent to provide water for the Fire Service in case of burst water mains. Its stagnant waters were never used except as a place to dump the bodies of dead dogs, cats and rubbish.

In the early years of the war the Northern Ireland Government failed to provide enough at raid shelters in the streets on the grounds that the likelihood of an air attack from German bases in France to such a far-off target was remote. The civilian population also grew complacent with the regular false alarms and the sound of the air raid sirens. This was to prove a costly error of judgement. The first major air raid occurred on the night of April 7, 1941 when the Luftwaffe attacked the dockside area of the city and despite all the previous alarms no sirens gave warning of their arrival. Worse was to follow. A week later, on Easter Tuesday night the German aircraft returned, this time with a larger formation. On that night 370 bombers left their bases in France and headed north. Because of weather conditions over Belfast only half succeeded in reaching their main target with the rest attacking secondary targets along the west coast of England. Their mission was to destroy the shipyard, aircraft works and munition factories. This time the air raid sirens gave warning of their approach but it was some time before the first pathfinder planes arrived to illuminate the city with the parachute flares. The reaction from the people of the streets of the St James's area like elsewhere in the city, was to seek shelter wherever they could as there were no air raid shelters in the vicinity. Some crawled under the kitchen table, others under the stairs where coal was stored. No one ventured out because it was felt that it would be more dangerous to be out in the open. In all the houses, the young and the old, huddled together and prayed. The ground shook as the bombs fell mostly in the north and east of the city. The nearest bombs fell on Beechmount 400 metres away causing the destruction of 15 houses and the death of three families. The air raid lasted for six hours and only at 5 a.m. was the all-clear siren heard. As the residents emerged into the morning light the sky was filled with smoke and ash from 200 major fires that were burning.

As a result of this raid, people began to wonder was this raid the first of many. A week later on the night of April 15, Easter Tuesday, at the sound of the air raid warning many decided to make for the Falls Park and the hills around Belfast while people from the Grosvenor Road streets and Roden Street headed for the Bog Meadows. From the St James's streets many hurried up St James's and Donegall Roads where they were joined by countless returning home. Everywhere and everything was covered in ash and dust. Throughout the following weeks, the sirens frequently wailed but no bombs fell. Then on the night of May 4, another 200 bombers of the Luftwaffe approached Belfast from different directions intent on destroying the aircraft factory, shipyard and the harbour. In addition to high explosives huge numbers of incendiaries were dropped causing large fires to erupt especially around the docks area. The reaction of the civilian population was to head out of the city. Once more I was pushed up to the Falls Park to spend another night out in the open air. The fire raids of May and the repeated air raid warnings that followed convinced my parents to register myself and my two brothers as evacuees under the govenment scheme aimed at encouraging parents to send their children out of the city to different parts of Northern Ireland. The result was that we ended up in the middle of the Armagh countryside housed with a farmer's family near Loughgall. There we stayed for several months enduring basic living conditions until things improved back home in Belfast as the threat from the air decreased when the Luftwaffe shifted its attention to the eastern front and the Soviet Union.

Figure 18.1 *US Army practising with bazooka in the Bog Meadows*

hundreds of women and children from the lower-Falls with bedclothes and mattresses strapped to prams and bicycles. Private cars headed out along with lorries and delivery vans. The author was among them strapped to a pram accompanied by my brother and sister. We headed for the Falls Park in which we were directed along the cemetery wall to of a large beech tree that afforded some shelter at least from the elements. Many went further towards Andersonstown to spend the night in the barns and sheds of Collin's and McGovern's farms.

From the high vantage point of the Falls Park one could see the flares and the tracers heading upwards in the midst of a huge ball of fire that covered the city. One of the wardens was a neighbour who reassured us that we were safe. We remained there until the early hours of Wednesday morning before

In late autumn 1943 U.S. forces started to arrive in the build up to the invasion of Europe and were billeted in different places throughout Northern Ireland. Reaction to the American soldiers was mixed. Some saw their presence as reinforcing Unionist rule but generally they were well received especially by the girls who flocked to the downtown dance halls to meet them. Some became war brides and ended up leaving for the United States after the war. Only on one occasion did they appear locally in any strength. The Bog Meadows was used by a company of American infantry as a firing range to test their anti-tank weapons. The particular weapon tested was called a bazooka that required two men to arm and fire it. The targets they aimed at consisted of three huge canvas images of the leaders of the Axis powers, Togo, Mussolini and Hitler placed out into the edge of the open water near St Katherine's Road. During the firing one of the loaders was injured by the recoil of the explosion and bled profusely from the wounds received. Needless to say, the targets were hit many times during this exercise! (Fig 18.1).

The Laharna 'Cinema'

The war years curtailed the movements of people in terms of travelling overseas or even across the water to Britain. Indoor entertainment was mainly confined to the home or to the cinema which flourished during the 1940s. The many 'picture houses' as they were called showed a great variety of British but mainly American movies. One had the pleasure of watching not one but two films for the one admission price, with the main feature film preceded by a forgettable shorter presentation. In between the two films, many cinemas also presented Pathe News or Movietone which, given the time, focused on war news. Such newsreels were history by the end of the week in which they were shown and were discarded.

One enterprising young man from St James's Gardens, Jimmy Cahill made use of these old newsreels in his own 'theatre' that was housed in a nearby air raid shelter. He borrowed a hand-cranked 35mm projector and two reels of old newsreels and set about preparing for the first show in what his friend and neighbour Noel Diamond christened the Laharna cinema after a place in Larne that he often visited. They both set off to Sandy Row to buy whitewash to whiten the back wall of the shelter on which to project the film. On their return they prepared the walls and organised the seating of planks placed on top of bricks and announced the date of the first 'premiere' to the local boys and girls.

The projected images of the newsreel proved popular with the viewers and most attended each nightly presentation even though they were seeing a repeat performance. But tragedy struck when Jimmy decided to check the film for breaks in the sprocket holes. Using the light from a 'holy' lamp that was normally placed under a religious picture, he held up the reel to check for any breaks. Unfortunately the candle set the film alight and the whole reel disappeared in a cloud of smoke and flame. It was ironic that the reel

Fig. 18.2 Children attending the first 'premiere' of Pathe News in an air-raid shelter.

that disappeared in a ball of smoke and flame contained footage of the fall of Mussolini and with it the end of the Fascist dream. Likewise the dream of a cinema in an air raid shelter also ended. The projector was returned minus one reel and the 'theatre' was given over to the production of plays.

Plays such as 'The Black Swan' were produced involving local children all anxious to have the leading roles. Rehearsals were carried out in the back gardens of the local houses. Disputes arose as to would have the role of the swan and the arguments persisted until it was discovered that the Black Swan was a ship not a bird! When the show opened in the 'theatre' it proved a great success for the young audience and other plays were planned. Jimmy and his friend decided to capitalise on the evident enthusiasm of all concerned by selling lemonade at one halfpenny per glass. After making a small profit on the first bottle of lemonade they went to the local shop to buy another but their request was refused because the shopkeeper considered them to be in competition!

The plays continued for some time without any refreshments until the Belfast Corporation thought it was time for the shelters to be removed from the streets towards the end of the war. The 'theatre' was demolished by the demolition firm of Eastwood and Sons and the bricks and concrete dumped in various places such as the rear of Corrigan Park in the Whiterock. Amongst the rubble lies parts of the 'screen' on which episodes of the Second World War were projected still covered with a film of whitewash!

CHAPTER 19
Wildlife in the Blackstaff Lowlands

A

B

C

A. BITTERN
B. BEAN GOOSE
C. IBIS

Fig 19.1 *The birds noted by John Templeton in the Bog Meadows*

ditches and hedgerows combined with the open expanses of water, mudflats and the absence of artificial fertiliser produced a number of different of habitats in which a wide variety of plants, birds and animals flourished. In summer the whole of the Blackstaff Lowlands would have been alive with insects of all kinds onwhich fed numerous species of birds including swallows, swifts and sand martins. In the evening hours, corncrakes would begin their rasping sounds which continued until morning. In winter, it was the winter-feeding grounds for wildfowl and waders, such as the snipe. In such cirtumstances it is not surprising that the earliest records of bird life in the Bog Meadows include reference to many species that are no longer seen in the area.

The earliest records are those of John Templeton (1766-1825) who was the owner of farmland on the Malone Ridge that stretched down to the edge of the Bog Meadows. He noted the shooting of a bean goose there in February, 1801, a bittern in January, 1811 and an ibis in September, 1819. (Fig19.1) (Deane, 1983)

William Thompson (1805-1852) was another naturalist who kept records of bird Iife in the Bog Meadows as well as joining shooting parties there in late summer. He mentions in his memoirs the shooting of snipe as well as birds that are long extinct in the area such as ruff and bean geese. (Fig. 19.2)

In more recent times, Robert Patterson (1863-1931) made a list of the bird species that he had seen which included kingfisher, whinchat, wood warbler, yellow bunting, water rail and woodcock as well as mallard, teal and widgeon. Despite the impressive list of bird species, he concludes that the whole habitat

In the past individual holdings in the Blackstaff Lowlands were criss-crossed with drainage ditches and devoted to pasture, potatoes and hay-making in the summer. The proximity of these fields to the town of Belfast would have encouraged cattle fattening for the nearby market and for the export trade. Hay was in demand in the town for the urban horse population as well as for winter feed for the cattle. In return, the farmers procured manure from the stables in the town. The lowlying nature of the meadows acted as a deterrent to settlement in the area. The only habitations lay on the approach road to the Saltwater Bridge, a collection of 'mean housing' along Sandy Row whose inhabitants benefited from living near the town as well as farming the small acreages available to them. The network of drainage

Fig 19.2 *The ruff, one of the birds that was considered long extinct by W. Thompson*

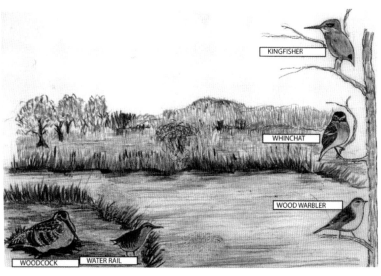

KINGFISHER

WHINCHAT

WOOD WARBLER

WOODCOCK   WATER RAIL

Fig. 19.3 *Some of the birds recorded by Robert Patterson (1863-1931).*

Figure 19.4 *The elusive Corncrake that in recent times was a breeding bird in the Bog Meadows.*

would be lost and 'the home of the snipe and wild duck will be transformed into desirable villa sites'. (Fig 19.3)

Douglas Deane alludes to the records kept by David Branagh of the Donegall Road who over three years from 1958 to 1961 noted 101 species on the Bog Meadows that was larger then than now. In these records are listed some rare species such as spotted redshank, green and wood sand pipers, greenshank, ringed plover and knot. He gives an amazing total number of different birds that over wintered including tufted ducks, golden plover, pochard, and whooper swans. By comparing the records of 1891 and Branagh's, Deane cites only five that were not present in the period 1958-61 which were the robin, whinchat, wood warbler, twite and barnacle goose. Even more surprising was the fact that in 1960, 50 species were found to be breeding compared to 20 in 1891! In his concluding remarks, Deane states that the wildlife is gone, the shooting of wildfowl is finished and the marshes have been drained to make way for an industrial estate.

Fortunately part of the Bog Meadows has survived as well as a substantial number of bird and plant species. In a survey conducted by the Ulster Wildlife Trust in 1989 it was found that 'despite the vivid display of urban expansion, this area, remarkably still holds examples of most of the original habitat types and a fascinating mix of plant, bird and insect species'. In a list of plant species, over 100 are mentioned as present, with a number dominant in the different vegetation typha: such as lady's smock, willow herb, meadow sweet, horsetail, buttercup, dandelion, bullrush and rushes. Marsh orchids are noted in the wetter areas.

Among the bird life surveyed, a large number were classified as breeding in the Bog Meadows. They included common birds such as magpie, starling, sparrows etc. but also numerous birds of the wet grasslands such as skylark and meadow pipits. Among the willow scrub were found the willow warbler and the stonechat. In the disturbed ground goldfinches and linnets were noted. The corncrake is mentioned but not conclusively as a breeding bird. (Fig 19.4)

CHAPTER 20
The Flooding Hazard

During the late 18th century and the early part of the 19th century when industry was beginning to expand along the Blackstaff, severe flooding occurred which affected large areas of the town. In 1775 "during a very high tide, boats plied for hire in High Street." (Millen, 1932) In January 1796 high tides again forced the waters of the Farset (and presumably the Blackstaff) back with the result that the south side of Arthur Street was under 13 feet of water. In 1838 Ann Street and Corn Market were flooded. Serious flooding also occurred in 1868 and 1869.

These events were the direct result of two centuries of exploitation of the natural forest of the lower Lagan valley and the surrounding hillslopes . Early maps reveal the existence of extensive oak forests. (Fig. 20.1)

Over time these were gradually cut down for all sorts of uses by the local landlords, merchants and tenant farmers. *"To the depredations of the tanners (for oak bark), charcoal burners (for ironsmelting), coopers, carpenters and shipbuilders was added the rapacious grasp of a rapidly rising peasantry"* (Evans, 1944) With the trees gone, the rain that fell flowed directly downhill into the numerous rivulets that previously did not exist. There was little or no interception by the grasses and shrubs that replaced the trees. The Blackstaff and its tributaries were swollen by the increase in the runoff from the surrounding land surface and the greater load. The natural embankments in the lower reaches of the river were unable to prevent the increased volume of water from breaking out to cover the low ground on both sides of the river with a veneer of sediment that together with the silt deposited from tidal waters collectively became known locally as 'sleech'. The trees that once grew on this low lying flood plain gradually succumbed to this continuous inundation changing the whole area into a series of narrow channels separated by low mud banks bereft of vegetation. Regular flooding of the lower Blackstaff constituted a serious risk to the life and limb of those who lived near it. In the early years of the 19th century this risk was low because few people had their residences near it. As industry and commerce began to grow in the markets

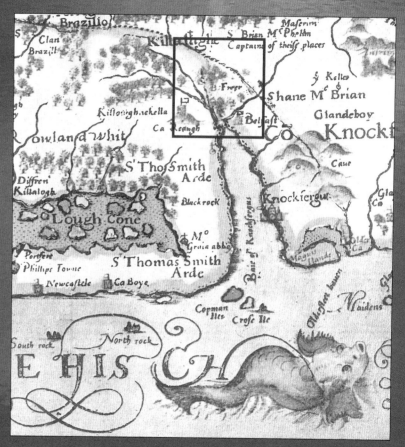

Fig. 20.1 Detail from the map of Ireland by Baptista Boazio, 1599 (source: the British Library. It shows the forested areas between the Farset River and the Lagan that provided a substantial resource for later exploitation.

area of Cromac and Sandy Row, people who sought work and housing in the area had to face the prospect of the river breaking its banks. Not only were they in physical danger from the rising waters but also from the pollutants that it carried. The Medical Officer of Health in 1852 refers to the area from the Linen Hall to Donegall Pass as suffering from ' the Blackstaff nuisance'. In his report he mentions the fact that the Blackstaff was badly obstructed by the weir at Joy's paper mill reducing the rate of flow of the river above that point. He also drew attention to the problem of sewage disposal during high tides. Tidal waters passed up the main sewers preventing the sewage from exiting to the Lagan. He notes that the lower parts of the district became inundated during high tides accompanied by high volumes of water coming down the river and the residents *suffer directly and immediately in health and property and long after from the humidity which remains'* (Malcolm, 1852)

He failed to mention in his report the danger posed by pollutants other than sewage. Along the banks of the main tributaries of the Blackstaff such as the Ballymurphy and Forth –Clowney Rivers were a number of bleach works and bleach greens engaged in the process of changing the natural brown colour of linen to white. To do so required in the early days potash and later sulphuric acid known then as oil of vitriol. Chlorine was also used. Copious amounts of water were needed and dams were constructed to ensure an adequate supply. The rivers were used to carry off the wastewater together with its chemical burden. In addition to the chemicals used in the bleaching process, the dye works at Milltown poured large amounts of dyes and mordants used in calico printing directly into the river.

Apart from industrial pollutants, the Blackstaff provided a convenient place to get rid of any form of refuse or unwanted material. Joy's Mill dam was also such a place. It became *'the receptacle of the refuse of upward of one hundred houses, besides factories and public institutions where many hundreds congregate and reside'.* (Malcolm 1852). In a remarkable prediction about the future state of the Blackstaff, O'Byrne cites the writings of a visitor to Belfast in 1810 who refers to a prophecy apparently uttered by one called Terence Dorne or Dorney. He wrote: *'Toe my goode Maistere Syrre Phalym O'Shayne - The daies shalle komme whenne ye stremme noue called Black shalle be blacke yndeede, when ye smelle of ytte shalle be so dystressfullie badde thatte ye mene*

of ye greate sytie heretoe grone shalle cause ye river to be covered uppe, for ye fyshese shalle all be dede, and ye stremme shalle not turne annye wheeles, and this shalle be in ye daies when ye shyppes shall be mayde withouten annye woode, and ye dwellings of ye folke shalle be lyghtenedde withouten annye candelles'. Little changed over the centuries considering that the Blackstaff was viewed as the most polluted river in the UK in 1970.

The flooding problem continued into the 20th century despite attempts to curb the rising waters by culverting the river from Great Victoria Street to the Lagan at the Gas Works in 1887. There was widespread flooding around the White Linen Hall and in 1902 the waters spread the full extent of the slobland. Flooding occurred periodically throughout the first half of the century and one particular flood almost lead to the death of the author by drowning.

I wandered down with other friends from my home in St.James's Gardens to view the river in full flood. Either by walking too close to the river bank or as a result of pushing each other about, I fell into the cold waters of the Blackstaff and taken instantly away. I hit the concrete edge of the bridge support and was swept underneath. I remember holding on to one of the concrete beams under the bridge but could not hold on against the current. I was dragged further downstream behind the houses that paralleled the river between the bridge and Broadway Road. I was then sucked under the bridge at Broadway and was swept on past the rear of the monumental sculptors workshop on the Donegall Road. By that time I had lost consciousness and was about to be carried further downstream beyond the view of anyone on the bank. Fortunately a passenger on a tram spotted me and told the driver who stopped the tram and ran down a side street where the river was accessible and jumped in fully clothed and waited until the current carried me down. He pulled me out with the help of the passengers and lay me down on the ground. By chance an auxiliary fire-service tender was passing and rendered first aid. I ended up in the Royal Hospital for Sick Children, the name of which is somewhat of an understatement given my condition at the time. I recovered after two weeks in the hospital and was at home when the driver of the tram called to see me. My presence was confirmation of his successful rescue for which he praised in a letter from the Transport Department.

SMART RESCUE IN BELFAST
Tram Driver Saves Child in the Nick of Time

While a tramcar was passing the Blackstaff River at the corner of Broadway, Belfast about 5.30pm yesterday, the driver caught sight of a five-year old boy, Desmond O'Reilly, of 20 St. James's Parade floating down the river. The motorman, James Smith, of 62 Vernon Street immediately stopped the tram, jumped into the river and succeeded in getting hold of the child. A number of auxiliary fireman, led by Fireman Walter Johnston, of a neighbouring Belfast fire services depot rushed to aid him, Johnston wading into the water to help to bring the boy to the bank.

The child was unconscious, but artificial respiration was applied and was successful. He was later removed in an ambulance to the Children's Hospital on the Falls Road where he was stated last night to be recovering from the effects of immersion.

Belfast Telegraph January 26, 1942

The flooding hazard reached epic proportions in 1952. The storm lasted for nearly two days, during which nearly 4 inches of rain fell. At the same time there was an exceptionally high tide (13.3 feet O.D.) and this prevented the waters of the Blackstaff from escaping fast enough to prevent flooding. In addition the volume of water coming down the Forth / Clowney River was so powerful that it headed southwards up the line of the Blackstaff adding to the waters coming down and consequently inundating the whole area to a depth of 1.5 metres. This reversal of flow was repeated in August 2008, resulting in the Broadway underpass being filled with 7 metres of water. These 1952 floodwaters changed the features of the Bog Meadows as much of the river banks and drainage ditches were washed away, so that large tracts of the Meadows became marshland and considerable areas became wide expanses of water.

The local residents were adversely affected. The storm began at 4.30 a.m. on the 9th August and by evening the floodwaters had overwhelmed the surrounding streets on both sides of the Blackstaff from Stockman's Lane to Cromac. To add to the problem of houses under water the sewers burst and raw sewage swirled around in the floodwaters reminiscent of events referred to earlier in the previous century. This caused the authorities to evacuate the districts affected, an operation which was carried out with the aid of the Fire Brigade and the R.A.F. using rubber rafts and a boat. Most of those from St James's area were lodged in St. Kevin's School and were cared for by Welfare officers and volunteers. By August 13th most people had returned to their homes to face the unpleasant task of clearing out the mud and repairing what they could but the dampness lasted a long time in the house foundations.

Residents from the lower St. James's Road area being rescued by RAF personnel in 1952

This air picture shows the area affected by the Belfast floods of Aug 1952. Key points are numbered - (1) Tate's Avenue Bridge; (2) Windsor Park; (3) Celtic Park; (4) Junction of Donegall and Falls Roads; (5) the water logged Bog Meadows and (6) City Cemetery.

Blackstaff rivers at Broadway. When the river waters reached a certain height at this point action was to be taken at the sluice gate, to hold back the river water from the Blackstaff. At Boyd's weir watch was kept on the advance of tidal waters from the estuary. These precautions were of limited nature and of little use in the event of a repeat of a sustained period of rainfall as had occurred in 1952.

The floods position was considered at a meeting of the Belfast Corporation Improvements Committee according to the Irish News, August 13, 1952. During the meeting the Assistant City Surveyor was instructed to bring detailed proposals for the construction of a culvert in the Bog Meadows as soon as possible. Mr Anderson told the Committee that 3.4 inches of rain had fallen on Saturday and Sunday, the 9th and 10th August. This was the highest recorded rainfall since records began, going back to 1914. The total quantity of water in the catchment area of the Blackstaff and Clowney Rivers was nearly seven million gallons, more than one-fifth the total water capacity of the Silent Valley reservoir! What was needed was a more radical engineering solution that would alter the whole basin of the Blackstaff and ensure that the floods of the past were never to be repeated. This question of what to do with the Blackstaff arose at a time when in the postwar years there was an increasing need for land for industrial expansion and new housing development.

Belfast Corporation decided over the short term to take some precautions in case there was a repeat of the flooding during the coming winter. Sandbags were distributed to the residents most affected and a dyke was constructed from Clarence Engineering Works to St Katherine's Road running parallel to St James Road. It was raised to one metre high and consisted of a rock core set in heavy clay. It was two metres across at the base and one metre across at the top.

At the Clarence Works where the dyke met the river the Corporation installed a sluice gate This gate was able to be lowered to prevent flood waters from coming down the Blackstaff. At two other points along the river the Corporation placed monitoring stations, one at Boyd's weir next to the Great Northern Railway goods yard and the other at the junction of the Forth and

CHAPTER 21
Development Plans for the Bog Meadows

The Bog Meadows were viewed by many including the Belfast Corporation as a waste of valuable space that should be drained and filled in to provide additional development land. The pressure to do so stemmed from a number of factors.

- The population of Belfast was constantly increasing After the Second World War the population of Belfast was around 400,000 and in need of improvement from the standard of housing in which many lived.

- After a housing survey in 1943 it became apparent that a large proportion of the housing in Belfast was unfit for habitation and should be knocked down to be replaced with new housing estates.

- There was limited areas within the city boundary for the building of large housing estates

- Belfast Corporation was alarmed at the prospect of industry going outside the city denying the Corporation of the right to levy rates on prosperous householders and businesses outside the city boundary.

- There was an urgent need to tackle the constant flooding which occurred along the banks of the Blackstaff with a comprehensive drainage scheme.

- Road traffic from the west and south was increasing and there was a need for a new approach road from the south.

The floods of 1952 forced the Corporation to embark on a major drainage scheme that was to transform the natural landscape of the Bog Meadows and end its isolation from the rest of the city. Such a scheme would also eliminate a constant but growing problem as residential areas encroached upon the Bog Meadows. The stagnant water in various pools provided a breeding ground for mosquitoes and the tipheads were infested with vermin. The Cleansing Department of the Corporation was forced to deal with this combined nuisance as more and more complaints came in from residents about the swarms of mosquitoes in the summer and the numerous rats running through the back gardens. Teams of men were employed in the early spring spraying the area with insecticide and waste oil that formed a film on the surface of the open water areas. Others were equipped with smoke cartridges and shotguns to flush out rats from the holes in the banks and shoot them as they emerged. Such efforts were designed to control rather than eliminate the problem so the prospect of a complete transformation of the Bog Meadows into an industrial and residential area was very appealing. (Photograph 21.1)

Photograph 21.1 Air photograph (1958) showing the Bog Meadows and surrounding area

The first stage involved the straightening of the Blackstaff from Stockman's Lane to the Donegall Road. The second stage required a relief culvert to divert most of the water underground from a point below the junction of the Clowney and the Blackstaff. This underground channel would follow a line under Ulsterville Avenue, Lisburn Road, Methodist College and Botanic Gardens to join the Lagan. It necessitated the demolition of a range of houses between Broadway and Celtic Park as well as the removal of a row of prefabricated dwellings at the Lagan Embankment. The remainder of the river channel from Broadway to the Gas Works was retained to satisfy those whose properties abutted the riverbank and who claimed riparian rights such as the Monarch Laundry. This channel was nevertheless deepened to increase the flow rate. Together with the effect of the new underground channel, it was expected that a flow of 1250 cubic feet of water per second could be accommodated to control any future floods. When the drainage scheme was completed it was planned to infill the whole area with domestic and industrial waste until the wetlands had been totally covered. A final cap of soil would retain some grazing land for cattle as well as providing open ground for leisure activities. To service the transport needs for the region, it was planned that a new Southern Approach Road would be built between Stockman's Lane and Donegall Road.. The City Surveyor's Report described the proposed development.

"For the purposes of preparing the estimate of cost of developing the Bog Meadows a tentative road layout has been prepared for an industrial area of approximately 150 acres between the railway and the proposed southern approach road, most of which is within the city. A smaller area to the south lying outside the city will be preserved as playing fields. Thus Stockman's lane, a residential area, will be separated from the industrial area. The land west of the proposed road should give space apart for education, part cemetery, the remainder of the area for playing fields and park. A small housing site could be provided along the Falls Road. The proposed industrial area includes land now the property of G.N.R. The acquisition of this will be by arrangement with the government."

Industry	*150 acres*
Housing	*20 acres*
Schools	*40 acres*
Playing fields	*55 acres*
Cemetery extension	*15 acres*
South Approach Road	*20 acres*
Undeeded	*40 acres*

This totalled 340 acres and 30 acres were to be set aside for the Transport Department of the Corporation. The proposed development would take eleven years to complete. The Corporation commenced negotiations right away to acquire the land. The local farmers opposed the development and the loss of their pastures. At a Planning Enquiry the legal team representing Mr McGovern and Mr Collins protested against the proposals. However, Mr Collins was willing to let the Corporation have 20 acres of the 59 acres sought whereas Mr McGovern showed an unwillingness to part with any of the 62 acres that were required. The Planning Tribunal found in favour of the Corporation and with the stroke of a pen the lands were transferred to the Corporation and compensation paid to the former owners. All that was preserved of their holdings was the family home and adjoining outbuildings. A few years later these were also to disappear as industrial and commercial enterprises vied with each other for property on the upper Falls Road and Kennedy Way leading down to the M1 motorway.. Only Pat Hughes carried on raising cattle on church land at the bottom of Milltown Row but even this small- scale enterprise ceased when the few acres of grazing land that remained were turned into playing fields for St Gall's GAC.

The demise of the last remaining family farms brought to an end an era when the fields on both sides of the Blackstaff River were actively farmed.

In these fields of natural wetland pastures and meadows hay was cut and summer grazing provided for fattening cattle for the market in Belfast but the proximity to the centre of Belfast and the problems of winter flooding convinced the Corporation that it was time to act to resolve the physical problems and turn the whole of the Bog Meadows into development land.

The culverting of the Blackstaff and the construction of the motorway bisected the Bog Meadows and cut off the western half from the Blackstaff. The construction of the motorway had other effects. It altered the natural drainage in the area, preventing water from the rivers from the west draining into the river and forming shallow ponds and marsh on the western side. It also enabled industrial and commercial development to take place in the eastern half because of the reduced threat of flooding. Boucher Road was opened up in the early 70s allowing development to take place on both sides until today when it has become one major commercial and retail area employing a considerable number of people in a whole range of operations from car sales to light manufacturing. The western half was subject to a different development strategy.

The Town Planning Committee of the Belfast Corporation decided in 1968 to go ahead in principle with the zoning of 37 acres of land for playing fields. These recreational facilities would consist of several all-weather pitches and a leisure centre that would be constructed on the Falls Road side of the M1 and would cover what was left of the Bog Meadows. In 1971, the Director of Education in Belfast switched the site of the leisure centre to the bottom of Tate's Avenue.

Initially, it was proposed that the land would be zoned for playing fields. Belfast Town Planning Committee proceeded with the leisure centre at Midgely Park on the other side of the M1 from the Bog Meadows. Twenty seven acres would be set aside for all weather pitches on the Falls Road side. However, the D.O.E. had other ideas and secured some of the land earmarked for playing fields from the Corporation with a view to turning it into an industrial estate.

This change of ownership and zoning was the direct result of the pressure brought about by the Action and Liaison Group of Voluntary Bodies of West Belfast. They argued that there was sufficient leisure spaces in West Belfast

particularly the Falls Park and it was more important to provide substantial employment opportunities for the area through the provision of industrial sites. One of the most vociferous opponents of the Ministry's intentions was Canon Padraig Murphy, Parish Priest of St.John's. He argued strongly at meetings with the Mr David Howell at Stormont against turning over the Bog Meadows for playing fields and pointed out the high levels of unemployment in his parish and other parishes in the Falls area. He accused the different government departments of discrimination against the Catholic population of West Belfast offering them opportunities to spend their time at play while the Protestant population on the 'village' side spent their time at work. He was exasperated with the further plan to build an overhead walkway across the M1 to allow the residents of the 'village' area to access the playing fields proposed for the Falls Road side. The net result of this pressure over several years was the abandonment of the plan to construct all weather pitches and the provision of a small industrial estate at Kennedy Way. Twenty hectares remained untouched as a small remnant of these once extensive wetlands. It was this wetland habitat and its variety of bird, insect and animal life that stimulated the formation of a local community group determined to protect it. A group calling itself The Friends of the Bog Meadows was formed to preserve and promote the site. With the support of the Ulster Wildlife Trust, they succeeded in convincing the Urban Affairs Division of the D.O.E. to conserve and enhance the natural resources of the Bog Meadows and Milltown Glen as one of its Urban Wildlife Projects.

The Ulster Wildlife Trust was commissioned to carry out a number of ecological and development surveys on behalf of the D.O.E. In 1989 they put forward a number of recommendations that included the following:

• An urban park to be developed as a nature reserve
• A crannog to be constructed in one of the open water areas
• An interpretive centre

The Belfast Urban Area Plan 2001 acknowledged these recommendations and identified the Bog Meadows as a nature reserve and landscape wedge for amenity and recreational purposes. It paid tribute to the support from The Friends of the Bog Meadows and the Ulster Wildlife trust. It was the stated intention therefore of the D.O.E. to acquire land in the Bog Meadows and Milltown Glen to further these aims.

In order to conserve the remaining insect, bird and animal life it was proposed to build an encircling moat by widening and extending existing water- courses. In addition to recreational use, it was also the desire of the D.O.E. to encourage school children to visit this habitat by constructing a field centre in the Milltown mill area. Refreshments and toilet facilities would be added later in areas that would be non-intrusive on the environment. Other undertakings included

- Along the western edge near the boundary with Milltown cemetery, a soft, red sandstone cliff face would be exposed to encourage the return of the sand-martins.
- Hedgerows would be introduced along the lines of the old field boundaries
- A nature trail would be laid down
- A children's play area would be constructed at St Katherine's Road
- At a later stage, an arts, heritage and genealogical centre would be opened centre in the Milltown mill area.

The Bog Meadows Initiative as it was euphemistically called by the D.O.E. promised much but accomplished little at the start. It succeeded in financing further ecological studies, funded the negotiations over the acquisition of church land and acquired small plots of land in Milltown Glen included the cottage at the bottom of Milltown Row. When funding was withdrawn it succeeded in alienating the FOBM and other consultants by the stop-go nature of the project and by prioritising other similar projects elsewhere in Belfast.

At the end of the 90s, the Bog Meadows Initiative was given a new lease of life when grant aid from the European Union Special Support Programme for Peace and Reconciliation, and with the help of the D.O.E. Rivers Agency and Environmental and Heritage Service led to the purchase of the site for the Ulster Wildlife Trust. With its future secure and a management team in place, the twenty hectares under this new jurisdiction has seen a number of development initiatives since including;

- Reinstatement of the hedgerows along the former field boundaries
- Introduction of cattle to replicate the period when the land was meadowland
- Establishment of nesting sites for birds such as the sandmartin
- Maintenance of open water areas for wildfowl
- Encouragement for schools to visit the area

The Bog Meadows as a consequence was reduced to a mere fraction of what it had been previously. The reduced size of the Bog Meadows and the changed physical conditions impacted upon the bird life but many breeding species have survived and the site provides a feeding ground for many migrant birds.

The Blackstaff River has finally disappeared from its original line as the last section of the river was covered over as part of the road developments along the M1 and West Link in 2007. It brings to a head the various attempts to control it over the past two centuries and confine most of it to a hollow steel and concrete shell. Its role in shaping the nature and extent of the Bog Meadows is now confined to history. Its importance in providing water power for the early industries along the tributaries has ended and its course can only be deduced from its tributaries or as a red line on the maps of the Rivers Agency. In an age when global warming threatens an advance of the seas around our shores, it is perhaps prophetic to suggest that the tidal waters of Belfast Lough might once again encroach upon what is left of the Bog Meadows and reclaim the land that was once covered by estuarine waters some 10,000 years ago.

The River Blackstaff with the Clowney appear to have reclaimed their former course by flooding the Broadway underpass, at the end of the M1 motorway, on 16th August 2008.

BIBLIOGRAPHY

Baket, J and Kerr, R. *Snapshots of Belfast, 1920-1929.* Glenravel Local History Project, Belfast, 1994.

Bardon, J: Belfast, *An Illustrated History* Blackstaff Press, Belfast, 1982.

Bardon, J and Bernett, D. Belfast, *A pocket history.* Blackstaff Press, Belfast, 1996.

Belfast Newsletter, 3.3.1786, 15.6.1792, 26.5.1797, 18.4.1809, 9.2.1813.

Benn, G. *A History of the town of Belfast from 1789 till 1810.* Marcus Ward, Belfast, 1880.

Brodie, M.(ed) *Irish Football League, 1890-1990.* University Press, 1990.

Carleton, T. *Heads and Hearths: The hearth money rolls and poll tax returns for Co. Antrim.* Belfast, 1991.

Cleary, P.G. 'Spatial expansion and urban ecological change in Belfast with special reference to the role of local transportation 1861-1917'. Unpublished Ph.D thesis, QUB, 1980.

Deane,D.C. *The Ulster Countryside.* Century Books, Belfast, 1983.

Evans, E.E. 'The site of Belfast', *Geography*, 22 (1937); 'Belfast: the site and the city', **Ulster Journal of Archaeology,** 3rd Series, 7 (1944).

Fleming, G. *Magennis VC.* History Ireland, (1998).

Good, J.W. *Ulster and Ireland.* Maunsel, (1919).

Harbinson, R. *No Surrender: an Ulster Childhood* (Faber & Faber, 1969; reissued by Blackstaff Press, 1987).

Jones, E. *A social geography of Belfast.* OUP, 1960.

Kinealy, C. *Customs, Courtship and Conflict: May Eve Celebrations at the Bog Meadows.* Belfast, 1990.

Longley, M. 'Letters' from *An Exploded View* (Victor Gollancz, 1973).

Malcolm, A.G. *The sanitary state of Belfast.* Paper read to the statistical section of the British Association (1852) and published by the Belfast Social Enquiry Society.

Mac Aodha, B. (ed) *Topothesia: essays in honour of T.S. O Maille.* Galway, 1982, Translation in Hughes, A.J. 'Deirdre Flanagan's "Belfast and the placenames therein", **Ulster Folklife, xxxv iii (1992).**

McKeever,P.J. 'A Story through Time'. *The Foundation of the Scenic Landscape of Ireland (North),* **Geological Survey of Ireland, Geological Survey of Northern Ireland.**

Mitchell, F. and Ryan, M. *Reading the Irish Landscape.* The Town and Country House Publishers. Dublin (1997).

Moore, A.S. *Old Belfast.* Belfast, 1951.

Muir, A. The eighteenth-century paper makers of the north of Ireland. **Familia, Ulster Genealogical Review, No 20, (20).**

O'Byrne,C *As I Roved Out.* Irish News, 1946; new edition, Blackstaff Press, 1982.

O'Laverty, J. *Historical Account of the Diocese of Down and Connor,* 5 vols. Duffy and Sons, 1895-8

Reeves, W. *Ecclesiastical antiquities of Down, Connor and Dromore, consisting of a taxation of those dioceses, compiled in the year 1306.* Dublin, 1847.

Radford, M. 'Closely akin to actual warfare'; the Belfast riots of 1886 and the R.I.C.. **History Ireland,** Vol. 7, No. 4, Winter 1999, (27).

Scott, R. *Wild Belfast.* Blackstaff Press, 2004.

Young, R.N. (ed.) *Historical Notes of Old Belfast and its vicinity.* Belfast, 1896.

Whitworth, R. 'A plan of part of the River Lagan and of the intended navigable canal from Lough Neagh to Belfast surveyed by the Right Honourable the Navigation Board of Ireland', 1768, scale 2 Irish miles to 3 inches, PRONI, T1763/8